THE PASTOR'S

SOUL CARE

ENRICHING THE INNER LIFE

Published for Mark Ryan by Verite CM Limited

Printed by Verite CM Limited
Worthing UK BN12 4BG

www.veritecm.com

ISBN 978-1-910719-96-1

Visit www.pastorssoul.com

Dedicated to my Elim ministry colleagues who like ministers from all streams have worked tirelessly to innovate and had the courage to serve beyond their experience into the unknown. You have given hope for the dawn of a new day.

In loving memory of
Luchen and Jewel Bailey

Contents

Foreword

by Chris Cartwright

I once spent a day with Gordon MacDonald. In truth, there were 60 of us, pastors and church leaders who had travelled from across the globe for an intensive week of leadership development and mentoring. With over 40 years of pastoral leadership behind him and as a best-selling author and speaker Gordon MacDonald began with these words: "the toughest task you will ever have as a leader is to lead yourself." That one statement was worth the air fare. I remember the remainder of the day as nothing short of a download of wisdom, insight and revelation into my heart and spirit. I had gone to the Conference seeking to learn how to nurture, encourage and lead others. I began to understand that God wanted to do far more than that; He was speaking deeply and personally to me about my own heart and soul.

> "the toughest task you will ever have as a leader is to lead yourself." That one statement was worth the air fare

When an experienced leader speaks like that it can be Life changing. Mark Ryan is such a leader. Grounded in years of pastoral experience in the US and the UK, in small, medium and large church settings, Mark writes with clarity and conviction, passion and purpose.

Mark has a deep commitment to the church and to church leaders. He is one of the most generous Church leaders I know; spending time, sharing resources, investing relationally and working practically to encourage and develop other leaders. I'm not surprised therefore at the content of this book. What surprises and stirs me is the intent.

I'm reminded of the Apostle Paul writing to the church in Romans 1. Paul is writing to a church that is now spreading out in Rome itself. It's a church that he prays for "without ceasing." He continues, saying: " I long to see you, that I may impart to you some spiritual gifts to strengthen you, that is, that we may be mutually encouraged by each other's faith."

Paul literally wants to put something into them to build them up, to help and strengthen them. More than information, the motivation is impartation.

Mark writes with an urgency born of a loving concern for pastors that has clearly moved him. He wants to put something into us not from some great height of expertise but from the ground level of shared calling, shared challenge and shared Grace.

The fact that this book has been written during a global pandemic where every pastor in every context of ministry and mission has been stretched more than ever before gives it added relevance and application. Beyond a few extra ministry tools and adjusted devotional rhythms, Mark's passion and prayer is for every pastor to experience a deep wholeness, wellbeing and lasting renewal as they learn afresh to take care of their own soul.

Chris Cartwright
General Superintendent,
Elim Pentecostal Churches.

Preface and How to Use This Book

The Pastor's Soul Care came out of some deep conversations and concerns. In some ways the feelings I have in writing it range from being like an over-anxious parent watching their child's football match. Cheering them on! Hoping they do well. In another way, I feel like I am standing in the middle of the battlefield, pressing in with comrades for the final push of a battle we are about to win. I see heroes all around me. I have seen victories and casualties in this season. Both come at a cost to the inner life of the pastor.

This book is about the inner you. I have used the word soul to represent the real you, the inner you, the part of you that is you when there is nothing else left. It's that part of you that is cherished by the ones who love you. I have used the word soul to mean that part of you where your motivations and inner drivers sit. It's the part of you, that if neglected, everything else begins to fail.

This book is not indented to be the last word on the health and the wellbeing of pastors. ***But it is meant to be a timely word.*** I hope that it gives you pause to revisit some things you already know and some fresh approaches to achieve them again. I have made a real attempt to combine encouragement with practical application and some methods to try, in the hope they work for you.

The composition of this book is in itself a model of a deep conviction that runs through it, namely: You cannot travel alone. Your soul needs companions who speak life into you. So, this book is written with my friends. They are among the people whom I look up to and regularly receive input from. I look across at their ministries and marvel at their creativity and resilience. They have written a series of blog sized lessons that you can read as quicker input as you use this book. What they have said in a shorter space will give you deep thought on how to invest in yourself. Use their input to punctuate your day with the wisdom that comes from practitioners who have proven their ideas and lived them out in real life.

There are several ways that you can use this book. It can be taken away on a spiritual retreat and pondered over in prayer conversations. Another very helpful way to use this book would be to meet with ministry friends regularly for a season and discuss its contents one chapter at a time.

An important feature of using this book is to do the exercises in the 'thoughts for reflection' at the end of each chapter. Write your reflections to the questions set in your journal or notebook. In each of these sections there is included a bible passage or incident that speaks to the wellbeing of you as a pastor or leader. The idea is that you use these passages to write a message or bible study of your own so that you can teach any lessons you might feel your congregation or audience need to hear. By crafting your own message from these passages, I believe God will speak to you beyond what is written in these pages. There will be people who need to hear your wisdom and revelation from these biblical incidents and passages.

For free downloads of all the resources mentioned in this book please visit the web site **www.pastorssoul.com** You can have unlimited access to the resources. Please use them for yourself and distribute them to those whom you might think they would be of help to. The web site will be updated regularly for more resources.

Some people have asked me why I have used the term 'Pastor' so much in this book. They have pointed out that by using the word pastor others with different ministry gifts might not want to engage with the content. They wanted me to use the term leader. This, they argue, would add a covering to all ministry gifts. I have actually used the term pastor and leader interchangeably throughout. I deeply respect there are many other ministry callings and gifts that are not fully described by the word pastor. These people also need to be cared for and care for their soul. True. But I used the word pastor because I wanted to remind everyone who is involved in ministry of two important things.

I wanted to remind everyone in ministry of whatever shape, that part of any ministry involves caring and pastoring to some and at least themselves. So, if you don't see yourself as a pastor to many, or in any official capacity as a pastor, - you are a pastor to at least yourself, and those around you whom you love. I also wanted to remind everyone in ministry, that they have a 'Great Shepherd' who cares for them and their soul. You might not call yourself a pastor, but you do have a Shepherd. Your soul belongs to Him and He is your Pastor. Please use this book to partner with Him as you seek to care for your own soul in your journey of ministry.

Mark Ryan 2020

Chapter One

The Pressure Valve

Sitting in the restaurant for my birthday meal, all was going well, but there were several things detracting from the joy of the celebration. It was pleasant, but the backdrop to the occasion was becoming increasingly uncertain. Like many other pastors at that time in mid-March 2020, I was concerned that earlier on that day we had seen a significant drop off in people gathering at our church. People were absenting in the face of the imminent national lock down. We were not quite sure what was going on and how severe the pandemic would be. We were not sure what our response should be. My wife had a medical procedure looming and there were other medical issues in our family that were playing on my mind. My WhatsApp buzzed, and breaking our meal together rule, I looked at my phone. My friend had just suffered what proved to be a fatal heart attack. In the following few days the government locked us down and as a church leadership we were concerned about our ability to livestream and produce any sort of online response. We brainstormed and came up with a plan to use our church building as a base for our live streams and the following week we put something together and got it out there. What a relief. We were going to have to learn and upskill fast. As the lock down took hold my wife had to stay at home so that we kept to the lockdown rules. Little did we realise we would not attend church together as a couple again for the next six months.

The congregation applauded us for how well we coped, but we found it nerve wracking at times, not really knowing what we were doing. Privately I was in the fog of being in grief. I thought my wife might have something serious. I was unsure of the effect of the online meetings. Just a few weeks into the season of the pandemic another pastor friend, whom I was mentoring, was also lost to the disease. Like me, you too will have your story. You would have had to home school or deal with the disappointment of teenagers and exam results; care home losses and congregations that might have drifted; endless upskilling and technical glitches and separation from family; postponed weddings and funerals that just weren't what you imagined they would be. We have all had to dig deep.

There have also been many positives during this season and one of the ways we can care for the soul of the leader is to be intentional about calling out these unexpected lessons. But one of the things I have realised is that I had to learn how to release the pressure. We all need a pressure valve. We all need to know what turns the dial when the pressure builds. Some leaders have already developed pressure releasing mechanisms built into their routine so that they are able to carry on, but others may struggle to find the right outlet for this pressure. This book is about finding out the pressure valves so that pastors and leaders can recognise the build-up of pressure, and then more importantly, understand how to release it in healthy ways.

> **We all need a pressure valve. We all need to know what turns the dial when the pressure builds.**

The need for soul care for the pastor is becoming increasingly more evident. According to the Barna research group, the emotional well-being of pastors is down. They report it in stark terms,

> "Now, one in five (20%) say their emotional well-being is below average or poor, and those who are faring excellent or good now sit 15 percentage points lower than just a few months ago (50% vs. 65%). This is 10 times lower than data presented in The State of Pastors , a 2016 Barna study which found only two percent of pastors ranked their emotional well-being as below average—none rated it as poor—while the majority (85%) said it was good or excellent."[1]

It will be true of other caring professions no doubt, but the need for pastoral care to the ones who lead and give care is becoming an increasing feature of this season. There are clear warning signs that our soul is in need of some inner enrichment. Here are some of them. Please note if you have any of these:

- Lack of focus.
- Continual tiredness.
- Lack of motivation.
- Highs and lows of mood.
- Not being able to laugh at oneself.
- A critical or cynical spirit.
- Over sensitivity to criticism.
- Continually wishing you were somewhere else.
- Continually working from a place of worry that things are not going well.

---

[1] https://www.barna.com/research/andy-stanley-offering-clarity/

- Making some goals more important than they should be. This applies to leisure goals, such as 'I must bring my golf handicap down' or professional goals such as 'I must make sure I teach all the new series of bible studies'. The key is to ask 'why are these goals so important?'

These are all warning signs that you as a leader are beginning to need some soul care and inner enrichment. All of us need to identify how to release pressure, but more importantly for the long term, we need to find the root causes that allow things to build up.

When we see a list like this and admit that we identify with several things on it, we probably think we need professional help. For some this will be true. In fact one of the underlying themes of this book is that WE ALL NEED HELP! So let's never be afraid or ashamed to admit it, but let's start the journey of self-care together. There are things you can do yourself to help yourself. There are some things you already know to do and there will be things in the following pages for you to try in order to give you a new strategy of soul care.

One of the first insights to recognise is that you already know some of the solutions to your soul care. When you stop and step back in one of your quieter moments there is probably a repeating thought that you need to pay attention to. There may be a health direction that you have possibly been ignoring or not seeing as important. But actually, you know it. You just have not done it yet. You need to listen to what you already know, whether it's the voice that tells you to go to bed earlier, or eat less, or take your time on a project or talk to your children more. Whatever it is, it's time to listen to your own self. It's here where you will start. When you don't do what you know you should do, pressure builds and as pressure builds, even if it is subtle, it begins to wear you down and erode your resilience.

> There may be a health direction that you have possibly been ignoring or not seeing as important. But actually, you know it. You just have not done it yet.

As we journey together, as well as listening to yourself, we will learn together from the strategies and insights of others and what they have found to be helpful in enriching the inner self. Some of my friends who have vast ministry experience have contributed to this journey and we will hear from them in the later pages.

We need to add a layer of protection to our soul; caring for others, inspiring others, leading others, all takes something from you and you have to put something back. The idea of leaders' replenishment has been well documented over the years[2] and these ongoing practices will work in the long term. The focus of our journey together in these pages is not just ongoing replenishment but enrichment whilst under pressure that is not going away any time soon. This is not just a 'healthy practices' guide, although it is that, but our focus is more about doing things to deal with the pressure of an intense season. We want to offer some 'cannot do with outs' and 'must do's' to make sure that you are functioning well in a difficult season.

---

[2]Replenish: Leading from a healthy soul. by Lance Witt is a good example and healthy resource.

Maintaining our spirituality is vital and although we are going to assume it, it's worth saying that enriching ourselves spiritually underpins everything else that is offered in these pages.

When we talk about 'putting something back' after we have given out, this happens in the first instance and primarily by receiving from God continually. If this communion with God falters, many of the other things in this book will only have limited impact. Pray, read, receive, muse, meditate, or whatever you do, but do have some time where you engage spiritually in whatever style that is best suited to you. If you are depressed this will be more difficult. Actually, a sign of ministerial depression is that the time a minister attempts to spend with God becomes just moments of despair or completely unfocussed. If this is happening to you, the next chapter on talking to someone will be a starting place to help you. But however ropey or frayed it is, your time in God's presence is going to be one of the things that will bring you through any difficult season. It is what underpins any other healthy practice, as David says in Psalm 27: 5 *"For in the day of trouble he will keep me safe in his dwelling; he will hide me in the shelter of his sacred tent and set me high upon a rock."*

But let us define this idea of spending time with God because some will try to make it a rule of time, which leads to an unhelpful pressure. Here is the key: **Spend enough time until you know that you have received something, and your thoughts are fed.** Obviously, you might spend more time worshipping and communing deeper, but as a benchmark **stay with God until you feel that you have got more than when you went in.**

So, let us begin a journey of soul care for pastors and church leaders. It will take honesty to admit that there are some things to attend to. But let us remember the vast resources of grace that we have at our disposal, as the book Romans reminds us *"how much more will those who receive God's abundant provision of grace and of the gift of righteousness reign in life through the one man, Jesus Christ!"* (Romans 5:17). We readily accept that provision is worked out and applied rather than automatic, but let's stay in the knowledge that provision is there for us and God's grace will prevail for our leadership and ministry.

As we step out, let's move with two simple commitments: Keep spending time with God and listen to what is happening on the inside.

> Perhaps this is a new definition of prayer: Spend time with God – listen to the promptings of your inner self.

As you process these inner thoughts through scripture you will come to a place of direction on how to protect your soul.

Thoughts for Reflection

- Is there something that you have thought would make things better for you for a while, but you have been ignoring it? Write this down.
- What was the last, best and most uplifting thing you felt God say to you?
- **Read Psalm 27**...slowly.

Chapter Two

Don't just walk the walk, talk the talk!

As pastors and leaders, we talk for a living. We are the wordsmiths of the airwaves, in meetings, and in writings. Words are our tools. We are on the phone, in huddles, mentoring sessions, preaching and teaching scenarios. Hopefully we include a generous proportion of listening as well, but we do talk, and our words convey our vision of how we imagine lives can be different. Our words matter and they are important. When we talk, we present ideas, we coach, console and encourage others. We plan and work out problems through talking. Far from being a negative thing, our talking is often necessary.

But let me ask you a question.

> In all your talking, do you have anyone whom you can talk to? Is there someone who listens to your heart and mind?

Are there people in your life, not necessarily many, but who are there consistently, with whom you have conversations and a fair exchange of personal ideas? Talking is one thing, conversation is another. Conversation involves sharing. Not just talking, but listening and feeling. It's an interchange of ideas, of heart, or of emotion; but it is an exchange, it's not one way. Who is there that does this with you? If you are going to care for your soul, you need to have some people in your life you can talk **with**.

Because most pastors or church leaders talk to many people, they quickly gloss over this saying something like, 'of course I talk to people'. Because we talk on deep levels to people in need, we think we are sharing heart, but often we are just sharing care. Pastors can actually talk much but at the same time be incredibly lonely through lack of conversation that is a fair exchange for them.

There are different types of talking and we need them all. We need chit chat. Some call this small talk, or general conversation. Just chatting communicates to others that you value their time. To spend time without any agenda other than friendship or togetherness, also communicates high value to them as a person. You need people who are prepared to do that with you. They don't want anything but to simply spend some time talking about anything and everything. Having a little chat is more of a message than you think. Have you ever met someone with whom you could never imagine having a chit chat? I guarantee you are not close to that person.

We need information talk. Where people tell us facts or the detail of something. This communicates care and strength to us especially if we need the information to then go on and make a decision. Information is power to act and withholding it puts people in a vulnerable position if they need that information. We need this type of talk. Of course there may be protocols about when any information can or should be shared, but always have people in your life who give clear information.

Who is it around you that you can depend on to do this? As a care giver, you too need to be a clear information giver. It helps people. Some pastors like to hoard information and find power in not sharing to the ones who need it. This is a bad habit.

We need opinion sharing talk. This goes beyond information sharing to how someone might see the future working out, or what they see as important. Opinion sharing is important because it reveals values. You can never fully work with someone or trust them unless you know their values. You cannot be trusted unless you share your opinion. Timing in sharing opinion is important. This takes wisdom, but being afraid to ever share your opinion will always keep you at a distance from others, particularly your leaders. Sharing your opinion and being opinionated are two different things. Not every battle is yours and not every preference needs to be voiced. You do however need to voice your opinion because it represents what can be called your 'inner voice', or the real you. If you never reveal this, your soul shrinks and you don't grow. Face the fear of rejection and find the value in your inner voice. Even if someone rejects your opinion you might find that they actually appreciate you for sharing it.

We need heart to heart talks. This is more personal; it involves trust and is therapeutic to the future journey of our lives. Getting something off our chest, or sharing our hearts is like oxygen to the inner self. Over sharing with everyone is not healthy. Speaking everything in your heart wherever you can get an audience is a sign of an unhealthy soul, but sharing to the right person in the right conditions is a way of receiving life. We all need a trusted heart to heart with someone. Your heart is your wellspring, it is where the issues of your life sit. When this is locked, your life is locked. It is vital to your health that you talk your real issues through (Prov. 4:23). This is often in an informal and friendship-based conversation, but it can also be in a professional setting, which can literally be a lifesaver for your heart. Don't dismiss professional help. Heart issues run in themes and reoccurring thought patterns. When you have a reoccurring thought pattern that you don't know how

> **When you have a reoccurring thought pattern that you don't know how to navigate or they begin to dominate your inner life, it's time for a heart to heart.**

to navigate or they begin to dominate your inner life, it's time for a heart to heart. Not all patterns are problems. There are times when talking out an exciting vision means you are more likely to act upon it.

We all need advice, and this type of talk is like a mirror to reality. We all have a view of how life is, but good advice can show us a perspective on life, or even on ourselves, that can help us make the right choices. The bible actually says that we need advisors, "For lack of guidance a nation falls, but victory is won through many advisers" (Prov. 11:4). When a life has no advisors around it, there is always, without exception, trouble or detour. When we say advisors, we don't mean people who you can easily dismiss, we mean people whose voices have to be reckoned with. Advice is not just consultation or a talking shop, it is a strong strategic merging of thought that can sway a whole direction. Not all advice is to be followed but the process of hearing should make us more resolute as to why our intended action is going ahead. I have often found that even the rejection of advice modifies the way intended action is carried out in a better and more palatable form.

Here is the point, you need chit chat, information, opinions, heart sharing and advice type talk in your life. Every level and different type of talk has a function for you and others. Real soul care happens when you can engage in this. Notice that none of this talk is about presenting or communicating better to an audience, but your personal health.

Your soul is the very essence of you, it needs care. Don't ever feel like

> **Your soul is the very essence of you, it needs care. Don't ever feel like it's a luxury to care for your soul.**

it's a luxury to care for your soul. Because of the value of the inner you, it is important that we do not open up to everyone. The model of Jesus is that he operated in circles. He had an inner circle of three that never felt partisan or exclusive, but with whom he shared and who took on special assignments. He then had the wider twelve and so on out to the crowds. Who is your inner circle? Your soul needs them. Talk and relationship is a window of light that will bring energy to your soul.

This is important because to know and be known is vital to your health. This goes beyond the introvert extrovert split. To be known runs deeper than these personality categories. To know and be known is primal. This deep soul need came from the Garden of Eden (Gen. 2:18). Your soul needs to connect with someone, and someone needs to know you enough to touch your soul. Without this our inner life fossilises.

We get this at different levels, and of course, for those of us who are married it should happen with our spouse, although not exclusively. I have as a rule not to allow deep heart sharing, or anything I cannot tell my wife, with anyone else, especially those of the opposite sex. But you need friends with whom you can share. This brings strength to your soul when friendship is exchanged, invested in and valued. Too many of us bemoan the fact that we don't have real friends, but have you ever asked someone to be your friend instead of leaving it to pure chance connections and common interests? They can only say no, and if that happens it's probably a good thing for you! One of my best ever friends came about from him actively driving and meeting me and saying, 'Let's be friends'. We did not know each other at the time but that day started a very significant kingdom friendship for many years. If you want a friend, learn to ask then invest.

To be known and to know does not come exclusively from friends. We make a mistake if heart sharing is only done with those close to us. There are occasions when ministry colleagues, our leaders, or other professionals can speak into our soul as we share with them. This may only be occasionally, but be open to others speaking appropriately into your soul and not just your tight friendship circle.

I have tried to build a structure of relationships into my life that have supplemented the bedrock of my marriage. I always have someone in my life that I can look up to in respect, someone who I am inspired by. Then I have actively pursued friends with whom I can do some of life's journey. They encourage and reflect with me and hold me accountable to my promises. Then I continually have two or three people whom I am mentoring and helping in their life journey and ministry. I call this my Paul, Barnabas and Timothy structure. I always keep these three types of relationships. Each type of relationship does something for my soul. I am not afraid to ask or even call for someone new to fulfil these roles when life changes the make-up of my existing groups or circles.

Let's return to our question: Who do you talk to? Really, who do you share with? I mean really! The exchange of something from your heart is medicine to your soul. Landing an idea that is received by another, or receiving fresh insight from someone, is a cleansing agent for your spirit. If you want to care for your soul, talk to someone and have someone to talk to.

Thoughts for reflection.

- Do you have a Paul, a Barnabas and Timothy in your life? Have you intentionally named them, or do you leave it to chance?
- Would you contemplate asking for friendship? If not, why not?
- Talking and listening have to be in a balance but talking is a lifeline to your soul. List out who you can talk to at this moment. If there is no one, seek out a professional or a leader who can help solve this with you.
- **Read 1 Samuel 19:1-7** and reflect on all the conversations that Jonathan had and the function his talk played in the soul of the others in this passage.

Chapter Three

Filter to Focus

Settling into their idyllic Orchard Beech resort in Khao Lak, Thailand, Dr Maria Bennett, her husband Henry and their three children could hardly believe how luxurious the place was. It really was how the other half lived. They arrived on Christmas eve 2004 for a well-earned family holiday. The film, The Impossible, (2012) with lead actors Naomi Watts, Ewan McGregor and Tom Holland, catalogue for us the events that unfolded two days after their arrival. On Boxing day, without warning, many miles out to sea off the coast of Indonesia, was a massive under water earthquake, causing the now famous Boxing Day Tsunami. The overwhelming force of the tide swept far inland picking up houses, vehicles and people, carrying them along for many miles leaving devastation in its wake. There was no stopping it, humans were carried along like rag dolls, and in a moment lives and communities were changed.

There is another tsunami that has overtaken us, and with the greatest of respect to the people who were devastated by the Boxing Day Tsunami, this subsequent tsunami is global and all pervasive. Some would argue it is more dangerous. It effects all age groups and sweeps millions along in its subtle grasp. It is welcomed by some and hated by others and yet all of us swim in it. At times we love it because it offers choice and options as it carries us along. Like the Boxing Day tragedy, we are not sure where this cyber tsunami will drop us when it has finished with us. We are all caught in the ever-increasing tsunami tide of information and opinion.

Every single day our senses are assailed with messaging. Every hour we are invited to read a blog or see the latest news cycle. Every minute there is a cyber chain reaction that eventually finds its way to you and begs for your attention. We are carried along with the pressure of trying to take everything in but unlike the irresistible force of the Boxing Day Tsunami, we can resist the inevitable sweep of the information tsunami. If you are going to care for your soul, you have to apply a filter, or this tsunami will carry you until your soul is weary.

The saturation of your soul with information and opinion will have the opposite effect of feeding the soul, it will drain it so that you have nothing substantial to give. You have to filter. Particularly during the pandemic of 2020, pastors were inundated with opinions of what the future of the church would look like. Blogs, articles and You Tube films flooded the air waves to show us the way. Futurist books and prophecy angles began to follow, and the flood gate of information and opinion did not relent. If you, like me did not really have a strong opinion as to what might happen, there

> The saturation of your soul with information and opinion will have the opposite effect of feeding the soul, it will drain it so that you have nothing substantial to give.

was pressure to get one!

We all need to be well read and up on what is going on, that is a given, and the normal and regular disciplines of study and reading apply, but the frenetic jumping from one input to another has to be shut down in order for our souls to remain able to have enough for others.

This year I have changed my approach to how I use my spectacles. Instead of having one general pair of glasses for all occasions I now have three pairs for different scenarios. One pair helps me focus better when I am using my computer, another pair helps me see my notes better when I am speaking and teaching, and a further pair help me in general use. For some this would be too fussy, but the point is that there are different situations that require different levels of focus. During challenging seasons in our lives, we need focus more than at other times. We cannot coast as much when the pressure is on. But here is an important insight that might not at first be apparent, it is this and its vital that you catch it: **when we focus in a challenging season it releases pressure.** Rather than causing unhelpful intensity, focus causes a sense of progression that acts as a healing agent in your leadership soul. So, filtering out every opportunity to receive input is not a missed opportunity it is actually creating an opportunity for you to receive the things you need to hear for the present moment.

When our soul is weary, or challenged, our instinct is to seek rest and do nothing. Times of rest will be needed but if our time of switching off is followed by a complete switch on to everything that comes our way, then we waste our times of rest.

Here is a vital principle in soul care: **filter in order to focus.** Here is the reason this is important, because focus creates momentum and a sense of progress and progress heals the leadership soul. Filter to focus.

Let's take this idea of focus deeper. There are two

> # Here is a vital principle in soul care: filter in order to focus.

areas in which filtering will help us in our focus. The first is what we read, and the second is the voices we listen to. Let us add the caveat that we need to read widely and there is always room for fresh voices, but here is the principle of soul care: Read that which helps you and listen to the voices that inspire, instruct and enable you. Some pastors read widely, but hardly ever read something that they can apply that week. They are reading from the belief that everything they read will somehow be useful. But in seasons of challenge our reading has to be that which is useable. Long piles of books to tick off a 'must read list' is not feeding your soul, it's clogging your soul. Read that which helps you at this moment. Focus.

Reading to the mind is what exercise is to the body and so we are not advocating that we stop reading but that our reading is less general and more with a purpose. It has to be targeted to your current need. If your need is devotional and you need to hear enrichment for your spirituality, then read devotionally for a season.

There are three types of reading that will help. Devotional reading is reading that feeds you. Obviously, scripture falls into this category but there are other authors that will be a rich resource for you[3]. There is professional reading around

---

[3]For example: Developing the leaders heart by Dr Bill Lawrence. Carpenters Son Publishing

leading and decision making that will bring clarity to your approach this season. Included in this might be a look into the psychology of leading to help you understand the things you are going through or deciding.[4] The third type of reading is the 'what do you need right now' reading. This might not seem like a category but in order to care for your soul, read that which helps you. Stop reading things that are general and are just information fillers. Read to preach well, read to lead well, read to live well. But filter what you read. Read for leisure if that is what you need right now.

The same is true of the voices, or people, we listen to. They should be few and they should inspire, help and encourage us. The voices that we allow into our lives should spur us on to do something now and try some things that we find life in. Some of the widely heard voices can be overwhelming for some, if you are being overwhelmed or intimidated by a voice, filter it out. Even if all your friends love what is said but you just find it too much, filter and find the voices that help you. It's not wrong if you don't get into the popular podcast that everyone else is into. What is important is that you have the equipment to lead where you are. You don't have to do everything that everyone else is doing. Learning from others is one thing, being pressured to become an echo of another ministry is another. During the height of the pandemic of 2020 I decided that I was only going to listen to a Christian psychologist for a season, and sure I am certain that I may have missed out on some great insight from other leadership gurus, but I was able to gather my thinking in such a way as to help the team around me because I was not

---

[4]For example: The emotionally intelligent leader by Peter Scazzero. Zondervan
A little known work that is useful is The Emotionally intelligent Pastor by Jeannie Clarkson PhD. Published by Education and Clergy Development of the Wesleyan Church and Wesleyan Publishing House. A popular read – Andy Stanley's latest offering- better decisions fewer regrets Published by HarperCollins

cluttered with many different voices and theories.

There will come a new season where more general reading and fresher voices will be needed but for your soul care at the moment, give yourself the permission to filter. This is no different to not saying yes to every appointment.

Leading and pastoring is like learning to sail. Sailing a yacht has many variables and the weather conditions can change quickly causing us to have to react, but there are some basics that no matter where you are you need to abide by. This is why filtering and focussing is important. By filtering and focussing we establish routines and priorities that work for us even though we are out on the waves of uncertainty or in a changing situation. Because we are filtering what we take in we are actually giving good output from a position of clarity.

Without this permission to give ourselves a break from the tsunami of opinion, instead of leading, we begin to dispense sound bites. When we jump from one distraction or trend to another, we can fall into the trap of simulating leading our church or ministry instead of actually sailing it through the season we are in. A few years ago, I was on a break in the coastal city of Bournemouth, in truth I had pushed my schedule too far and for Kathy, my wife, this break was frustrating because I was falling asleep most of the time! Not good. One of the mornings we found our way to the pier. It stretches quite a way out into the sea, it is packed with attractions from a climbing wall, an amusement arcade, cafes, shows and even an adventure zip wire to take a thrill ride over the sea and back again! In one of my more fun moments we stood on the end of the pier and I simulated the scene from the film Titanic where Kate Winslet has her arms open on the bow of the ship clipping through the waves. 'Look I'm flying,' I said, to the only slightly amused

Kathy, as the wind and the spray from the waves blew against our faces. But here is the truth – we weren't flying because on piers you never move or navigate the waves or progress, you only get a taste of the sea and its conditions and then you can retreat to safety. On a pier you only endure a storm you don't sail through it and if the storm gets too much you can go and sit in the café and warm up. Pastoring and leading is not pier dwelling it's sailing.

When we don't filter and give ourselves the permission to focus, we fall into living on the pier where the distractions are many. Now and again, we taste the waves but because we are not filtering, we are not learning how to navigate them. We keep moving from one thing to the next. Our souls are distracted, and our souls are weary. Some might have thought making such a case for filtering what we take in was overstated, but the reason it is so important is because it will have a direct impact on how you are leading your ministry. The trouble with simulation is that it feels real, but actual progress is what your ministry and soul needs.

Let me change the scene dramatically. I was looking over Sydney harbour with the sun glinting off the waves, amazed at the amount of sea traffic that goes on there. I had just been taken to the heart of the city through the harbour on the sea cat boat that carries passengers from the suburbs to the city, what an amazing daily commute! Because Sydney harbour is a natural sea harbour it has many leisure craft and people learning to sail in it. It not how we imagine harbours in Britain. Our harbours are small in comparison. Sydney harbour is part of Port Jackson, consisting of the waters of Sydney Harbour, Middle Harbour, North Harbour and the Lane Cove and Parramatta Rivers. It is these different bodies of water that merge to make up the natural harbour of Sydney. The harbour is an inlet of the

Tasman Sea. It really is amazing. It provides close to real sea conditions without having to learn to sail on the open seas. We all need such places to train, and I am thankful for the people in my life who have given me a chance to experience what leadership is like without having the full weight of responsibility upon me. We all need these environments where we can learn in close to real situations, or in non-critical situations so that we can upskill and get use to what sailing is like.

But here is the truth- as much as the Sydney harbour can be a dangerous place and a high level of sailing skill can be attained, it is still not the open seas. Without a focus on what our mission is, what good routines are and filtering opinions that are not essential to us during an uncertain season, we become very skilled in sailing in over familiar waters. We might even say the waters and content of our ministry can become stale or shallow. We can almost navigate on automatic pilot, going so far and then turning back and heading for the calmer waters nearer the shore. It is enjoyable and the fresh air of the sea is all around, but it is still the harbour. People who live in the theory of the harbour say much but communicate very little value. In fact, as I watched this amazing harbour scene in front of me, I noticed one solitary yacht make its way through the snaking entrance of the harbour and quietly launch out into the open seas. Sailing takes focus and like pastoring or leading, without such focus we will only go so far, and if our soul senses we are not going as far as we should, it becomes jaded and in need of a healing touch.

To sail well you cannot drift or become distracted, there is information to help you navigate but you have to filter it so that your course is true. In fact, you are always going to have to keep the basic skills of navigation, sail trimming, boat and engine maintenance, weather watching, crewing and safety measures if you are going to sail well. The same is true of church leadership, there are some basics to always keep in mind and to keep going back to. Shepherding skills, disciple making skills, communication skills, team building, decision making skills, creative programming and planning and self-care and soul feeding are the basics of leadership. One of the best ways to navigate through a season of challenge, is to ask if what you are receiving is actually helping you in these skills. In all the material that you are receiving what is actually helping?

By helping we mean practical help that you can use. This is how you can sail through a storm, go back to your basic skills and refresh them. Filter and focus.

This book is about your soul care as a leader. It may not apply for every season in your life, but it is important for your soul care that you limit your input so that you can focus on what is needed. When you don't focus you become stressed, you become stressed because you have not given yourself the permission to only listen to voices[5] that help you through this season.

> # This is how you can sail through a storm, go back to your basic skills and refresh them.

There are many blogs and no doubt they will be helpful to someone somewhere, but after reading it for a few issues, if it is not helping, filter it out. There are many online conferences to attend, they are not all for you, especially the ones that ask

---

[5]Please refer to the appendix on signs that you might need a professional voice to help you.

you to be something you are not. What do you need to learn at this moment? Learn that. What would help you devotionally? Read that. Who would encourage or inspire you? Let that voice in. As for the rest, for now... filter so you can focus.

Thoughts for reflection:

- What are you reading and how is it actually helping in your daily life? Can you name the reason why it is helping you? Both professional and leisure reading can help in different ways, the point is: Is what you are reading giving you life and help? List what you are reading and decide.
- Who are you listening to? What did you use from what they said? How do you feel emotionally after you have allowed that voice to speak into your life? If you are drained, filter them out. If you are unmoved or not inspired, filter them out. Filtering applies to both in person or internet and podcast voices.
- **Read Exodus 18:** Focus on why you think Jethro was a voice that Moses could listen to. What attitude did Jethro display to make his voice a blessing to Moses?

Chapter Four

Key Relationships: Looking Closer

As a pastor or church leader you would have described this scene many times. But come with me one more time. Exhausted from the beatings and wearied by the questioning, and now stretched out and writhing in agony, the sting of the piercing of the nails sending fresh spasms of pain through his body, Jesus, hangs almost alone, and soon to be completely abandoned, on the cross. As he gasps for air under the weight of his body, in order for him to speak, he would have had to lift himself up in great pain to say something. We have recorded that Jesus speaks seven short statements from this position. To say what he said cost him more agony and so to say it must have been important to him. One of the statements seems to be about the house keeping of his own family, not particularly spiritual but for Jesus it was important to convey. This is what is recorded in John 19:26-27

> *Then Jesus saw his mother there, and the disciple whom he loved standing nearby, he said to her, "Woman, here is your son," and to the disciple, "Here is your mother." From that time on, this disciple took her into his home.*

Imagine in the last seven things you want to say, you use one of them to make practical arrangements rather than to convey the depth of your heart. But maybe if we look closer, we are seeing something of the depth of what was in the heart of Jesus. Conservative scholars will point out that Jesus as the oldest son in his family was actually obeying the Jewish law here in making provision for his family. So even on the cross Jesus was careful not to break the law, but that is not the full meaning of what is intended here. We know that he had not always simply complied with everything his mother wanted him to be, and he did not obey her every idea of what she might imagine he should do, (John 2:4). He also did not give her the privilege of family access when he was teaching, (Matt 12:48; Mark 3:33; Luke 8:21), so we know this statement from the cross did not come from just a sentimental moment. No, there is something deeper.

> The ones you can neglect and get away with it are the ones that are a key to a healthy soul.

When Jesus took care of his mother from the agony of the cross, he shows us that we all have key and familiar relationships right in front of us and these are to be valued and prioritised. We care for our souls when we care for the relationships that are right in front of us. One of the signs of our need of a deeper soul care is that we begin to look past or overlook those people who are travelling with us in life; wife, husband, children, parents, family, or close friends. The ones you can neglect and get away with it are the ones that are key to a healthy soul. We all agree with the need for care of these key relationships, but before you nod and agree, but don't plan to change anything let's take this deeper. Your soul care, and even a measure of inner healing, will depend on a deeper look.

> Your close relationships carry you as you also carry them.
> They deposit life and energy into you as you deposit life and energy into them.

There is a deep interplay in these relationships that is connected to your inner needs of security and acceptance. These close relationships are the house in which some of your needs live, are fed and thrive. When you have nothing to give, these relationships will carry you through a dry spell. There is a reciprocity about these relationships, but it is not always equal in giving and taking. Sometimes the balance is that you give more and there are other times because of your lack of health or angst, you take more. This is normal over the course of life so long as there is a healthy interplay. What these relationships can't handle is neglect, or mere routine, cohabitation or being taken for granted. In short, your key relationships always take work, and intentional care and input. So, if you have a healthy marriage, you have to have the intention to go deeper. If you have a good relationship with your kids, it has to become better and more nuanced. Every key relationship you have has to grow otherwise it begins to take life from you. In the worst case they drain or damage you.

Here is the danger for pastors, we often have above average marriages, at least on the surface. Our marriages have strong roles tied into our vocations, so we coast and don't work on them. We don't intentionally take them deeper, so our marriage subtly starts depleting our soul rather than feeding it. We give our kids church jobs and roles, which is totally fine, unless that is all you do. Our children begin to perform for us and our soul stops connecting with them.

Because our identity can easily become entangled with our ministry role, those close to us can begin to serve our role too much. We get can get caught up in working together and achieving a mission so that we cease to intentionally take these relationships deeper. In turn this lack of attention to the substance of our relationships leads us to maintain a false family life and order. Instead of us working

> **We need to stop propping up roles and invest in the person that is right before us.**

at these relationships so that they give us life, we begin to find our relationships are on the wrong footing, they are valued because they are useful to us for our role. This becomes draining to all involved because we are working at the wrong emphasis for these relationships. We need to stop propping up roles and invest in the person that is right before us. The danger is that our souls start getting life from other places. Our close relationships start shrinking in the influence that they need to have. We need to stay soul mates with those who are close to us. Detachment is a sign of our relationships being in the wrong place in our lives.

My younger daughter works on the ministry staff in a large successful church. She doesn't do this because I am a super Christian, she does it because God called her. I learnt that my role was to be an example but most of all to be Dad. When she was young, and I mean young enough for her to still want to marry me, she was asked at school to draw a picture of what her dad did around the house. The other children drew pictures of dads playing football, one was driving a car and others were doing various things with tools. My daughter drew a picture of me sitting at my desk with my books behind me studying. And then she said 'I put the phone there on the desk in the picture in case it rings' – pre mobile phone days! This was an early reminder that I was not spending the time I needed to with her, this was the picture of all that dad did. God used it to change me. It was a warning and I heeded it. Your role cannot give you what your key relationships are supposed to give you. Your role will give you lots of things, but it cannot be a soul's substitute for the people you are travelling with.

> Investment takes time and planning. It's something you do intentionally and don't just leave to chance, thinking it is happening naturally through proximity.

One of the important ways to care for your soul is to look at the relationships that are close to you and invest in them. They are the hardest relationships to evaluate, because they are so close, but they are the ones that when invested in properly will actually move you towards health. Investment takes time and planning. It's something you do intentionally and don't just leave to chance, thinking it is happening naturally through proximity. The mere fact you live with someone or see them often does not guarantee that you are investing in that relationship. If you are to care for your soul, you will have to invest in another close to you, that's how it works. God designed life as an interplay of giving and receiving between us. We have reduced this principle down to 'spend a bit more time' or 'take a break', both of which will be part of it, but investment in someone is more intentional and thoughtful. This is not a book about marriage and relationships but let us take a brief look at some key things that cannot be ignored if we are to go deeper in our close and key relationships.

Investing in your marriage.

We all grapple with what I call the Gordon McDonald principle. Basically, Gordon McDonald and several others have the rule that when they decide their schedule they first put in their commitments to their spouse and family and work everything else around this. There is no doubt that this formula is well intentioned and will work for many. If this is your method of family organisation and it works for you then please continue. The danger, as with all formulas, is that it becomes a lifeless routine of appointments and not real investment. So, for us mere mortals who might take a more flexible approach, in being flexible, we have to keep in mind that the real issue in marriage is to consistently prioritise time and to always communicate value. Time and value are the currency of the soul of any marriage.

Marriage changes over time and goes through different stages, as Pastors we all know this but then fail to apply it to ourselves! For those of us with older marriages it is really important that we communicate to our spouse that we still love them more and more and more, that our affection has not waned. This is particularly important because it feeds both the soul of the recipient and the giver. So, through which ever love language you have communicate that your love is still alive and kicking. Another vital investment for the older marriage is the element of mystery. When we get older, we have established likes, patterns, and routines, we even allow each other to occasionally take each other for granted. Although there is much security in this established order, it can become stale by assuming you know all there is to know about the person you have been with for all this time. Actually, this is not true, you don't know everything about your spouse because everyone grows and changes over time. You must communicate to them that you want to know them more and that you don't think you have them just sewn up in your mind. Break up your routine, have different conversations, ask for real opinions, and seek God for new directions. Older marriages still need mystery.

I have been amazed over my years as a pastor how younger marriage very quickly look like stereotypical older ones! Rapidly routines become rigid and cohabitation seems to be settled for. It's understandable with mortgages to pay and careers to be had and kids to look after. But young marriages need to have fun and be fun. Sure, life is not a constant party, but younger marriages feed off levity and can be dulled by too much brevity. Are you fun? I don't mean annoying silliness but genuine lifting of the other persons spirit to show

> **All marriages need proven trust.**

them that their value is not just in their economic contribution or childcare but in their personhood and company. Another important ingredient for soul care in marriage, both yours and your spouse's, is being responsible. This seems opposite of the fun part, but in the areas that need to be rock solid and dependable, being there and being consistent over time builds the indispensable ingredient of proven trust. All marriages need proven trust. To have shown yourself trustworthy in a marriage is vital. An atmosphere of unspoken mistrust is a killer to a marriage. It's in the younger years of marriage that this is built up. This goes for both sides in the marriage. You invest in your marriage by being responsible with the things that just need taking care of. My DIY skills actually stand for 'destroy it yourself', but I don't let things hang over the household because I don't have the skills to sort it, I make it happen through friends, relationships and hiring handy people, but it happens. It wasn't always this way, I would leave things without realising that unfinished projects or making do was actually not about the things, it eroded trust, and this cannot continue in a marriage. Young marriages need to have a track record of responsibility because this is the road to trust, and trust is the foundation you are building on. As you invest in your marriage, your soul is wrapped in security and your inner life is richer for it.

We are primarily seeking how to build your soul, as you invest in your marriage in these more thoughtful ways then you will have the feeling that your marriage has something that will last. This sense of longevity directly plays into your soul health. It becomes something you know you can count on. Marriage becomes more than just being together, but it moves to shared purpose and real desires. Invest to be blessed!

Investing in your children

Remember we are talking about your soul care, and the principle is as you invest in others who are close to you, your own health is progressed. This is never truer than it is with children of all ages, especially teenage children. Again, rather than the standard answer of spending more time with your children, although it is true that quantity of time with children trumps the so-called quality time every time, let us take our investment in them in a more insightful direction. There are two vital things you can do for your children that will also enrich your soul and theirs.

First parents need to always ask, 'what do my kids need from me right now'. I mean today and this week. Children have presenting needs and worries that quickly surface, and with help, quickly subside. Ignoring what they need right now erodes their sense of worth and builds guilt in your soul. Both of you lose. Your children might need organising, or comforting or instructing, or helping with a physical issue. There could be an underlying issue that you need to uncover but making sure their presenting and non-presenting needs are spoken into will bring health. But here is the key, as your children get older, you will not have the privilege of speaking into their needs on your terms but on theirs and in their time scales. One of the things I had to learn with one of my daughters is that she needed to talk things out but not until she was ready. So, my role was to say, 'when you are ready, we can always talk,' in practice what this meant was these talks often did not happen until nearly midnight! But that is what she needed and that is what helped, although I was tired the next day, I was richer on the inside. Invest in your children by being aware of what they need at this moment. This is more than constantly doing things for them, it is looking at their lives and seeing what they really need.

The second major way of investing in your children is to discover what motivates them, and then help to develop and refine those driving forces in ways that enrich them. Have you ever met parents who describe their children as chalk and cheese? Saying what worked for one just does not work for the other. This is because children in the same family can be motivated by different things and have developed different aspirations. Parents can fall into the trap of just smiling at this and thinking it is cute or quirky, but actually you can really invest in your children by taking these motivations seriously and working with your children to refine their motivation in godly ways. A child's love language can be material things, which might sound shallow to some, but children motivated by gifts can become some of the most generous adults and carers for the poor. It's as parents feed such motivations directing and refining them to be an advantage to their child's development and wellbeing, that makes the difference. It is worth repeating, spending time

Helping shape how they achieve their goals in a wholesome way is the prize of parenthood.

with our children is a given, but understanding where they are travelling and how they think they will get there is even more fruitful. Helping shape how they achieve their goals in a wholesome way is the prize of parenthood. This intentional investment into the motivational life of your children will do your soul good because it's actually a form of discipleship, and when we disciple others, we ourselves grow. It is also healthy because it reminds us that our lives are not the centre of the universe and other people have valuable aspirations that need attention. Children have dreams, and you can be an important key to those dreams. This matters to your soul.

Investing in friends or other close relationships.

Not all relationships fall into the nuclear family. Some of us have deep loving relationships that are with friends or wider family. One of the few places in the bible where friendship is overtly demonstrated is as the four carry their paralysed friend on a mat to Jesus for healing, (Mark 2:3-12; Matt 9:2-8; Lk 5:18-26). I often use this as a picture for when we are unable to pray, find some friends and their prayers will carry us to Jesus. But this story literally shows us one of the main functions of friendship, namely we are to be supportive. If we are to invest in a friend, we have to think through how we can be supportive to their job or role, that's what friends do, they lend support. This is important for soul care because we are specifically instructed that we are to carry each other's burdens (Gal. 6:2). The scripture takes this beyond being nice and decent and puts it into a spiritual principle of fulfilling the law of Christ. This takes it out of it being optional to something that is an expected kingdom principle. We need to broaden our definition of friendship from just having common interests to carrying weight on behalf of another. Our soul is like our body in that it needs to have exercise in order to be healthy, and it's when your soul bears some relational weight that it becomes healthy over time. Many pastors are good at shepherding but are not so good at friendship. We have many acquaintances, but friendship can escape us.

> **Many pastors are good at shepherding but are not so good at friendship. We have many acquaintances, but friendship can escape us.**

The other strand to real friendship is that we give and receive healthy, kind and honest reflection upon the things we are trying to do. It's the combination of true supportiveness and honest reflection that makes up the backbone of a friendship. The willingness to support even if it is not your way of doing things, and the courage to speak up when invited to in order to refine where a person is going, makes your soul stronger and richer. No one can live with a continual refining commentary on their lives and so real friendship is more supportive and generally waits for an invitation to speak. But for our part we have to build up trust with someone and always be willing to invite real reflection. One of my friends has literally shaped my career by having the courage to speak into a presentation that I invited his reflection upon. His input changed the way I approached the details of this piece and I believe the result was changed in my favour because of his advice. Who is supporting your life journey? Who is it that you trust enough so that you would invite them to speak into your situation? The clue of how to get this is obvious, go and be supportive to someone and invite them into your life. Your soul needs this.

One of the realisations that will come to you several times in your life will be that you will have to care for your inner being more than you think it needs care. At some point someone will take you aside and say something like 'why don't you take a pause for a little while and regather yourself?' Listen to when someone close is saying this to you because if you ignore them the doctor might have to say it to you! Eventually we all realise that life is less about what we do and more about who we are with. This is what soul care means, you care enough for yourself that you don't alienate the ones who are meant to be with you. The ones closest to you need this from you.

A few years ago, I worked on a police community reference group to help ease the tensions that had arisen in our city. For the rioting to subside some of us as community leaders met with different factions to act as community 'go betweens' and voices in order to try to help restore the city cohesion. The work was tense, delicate and involved many long hours. I received a call from the police one day to go to the police HQ and shoot a video to encourage the officers who had worked many hours on the streets under tough conditions. They told me to dress smartly in order to make the video the quality they wanted. I was happy to oblige as I felt all sides in the situation needed a boost. When I arrived at the city police HQ I was informed that we were not making a video, and they apologised for the ruse. After a briefing, we were taken by a bus to a local community centre where we were to meet Prince William and his wife Kate, the Duchess of Cambridge. It was a great experience, and the royal couple were well informed, genuine and supportive of the efforts we had made. It was one of those moments in life where you pinch yourself and think 'is this really happening?' On my way home from the community centre after we had been released from the security zone, I called my wife and had the 'you will never guess what just happened to me conversation'. I called my secretary, who was a Kate Middleton fan, and had the 'you will never guess what just happened to me conversation'. After these conversations as I walked home, I increasingly became aware of a growing sense of grief for my mother, who had died two years previously. This lasted for quite a while. She would have loved that I had got to do this, she would have listened and asked me over and over how it all was. She would have said 'well I never'. That was the phone call I really missed making. I had just come out of a really positive experience and I was sad. Not just sad, but really sad. The people who are close to you actually never leave you even when they are dead, so don't look past them when they are alive.

Thoughts for reflection.

- If you are married, ask your spouse what is one small thing that would improve the quality of your marriage. Work on it and achieve it by the end of next month. Do it straight away and make it a habit as soon as you can.
- What do your children of any age need from you this week? Is there something that has been going on for a while that you need to understand?
- Do you know where your friends need support? Ask them this week.
- **Read 1 Samuel 25.** Reflect on it. What can we deduce about Nabal's soul in the way he treated others? Why was he feasting like a king without even noticing his wife was missing? Is there anyone close to us who is having to make up for what we should be doing?

Chapter Five

Navigating Conflict

One of the most tragic occurrences in an ongoing military conflict is when it is reported that serving soldiers have lost their lives because of so called friendly fire. Friendly fire happens when an attack is launched on what is thought to be the enemy and yet it turns out to be troops or allies from the same side. It is often described as collateral damage, but it leaves a sense of defeat even when there is an overall win. In the church we actively and often knowingly engage in friendly fire. It just doesn't feel that friendly. It is this arena of conflict and the attempts to resolve it that can be so wearying and even damaging to the pastor's soul.

Conflict comes in many guises in the church arena. It can be subtle. Many pastors often deny that it is really a problem, ignoring it by being gracious for too long. Ignoring repeated patterns of passive or non-passive aggression only serves to pollute the culture of the church further. It can be an out and out challenge; it is often manifested in territories being formed and protected. Many churches have long since left having departments, instead these have formed into camps and strongholds. So long as the pastor doesn't touch these, he or she is safe, or so it might seem.

We need to be careful not to react to every failing that church members and leadership teams exhibit. People will have a bad day and do the wrong thing. That's what shepherds are there for.[6] When we are describing conflict, we are talking about repeated patterns of destructive behaviour that injure the mission or the people of the church. Don't react to the events but always respond to patterns. There are one off's that are serious enough in nature that we have to respond to, but sometimes even these, when you analyse them, have often been the result of an unchallenged pattern.

> When we are describing conflict, we are talking about repeated patterns of destructive behaviour that injure the mission or the people of the church. Don't react to the events but always respond to patterns.

Whether the conflict is subtle or aggressive, or simply non cooperative to where the church and your ministry is going, you have to deal with it. Conflict, in whatever form, is one of the hardest things that the pastor's soul ever bears. But here is the truth, unless you deal with conflict it will be one of the most destructive things for your inner health. Unresolved conflict

---

[6]If you have not read 'Lead Like a Shepherd' by Larry Osborne. (Next Leadership) please give it your attention. In this book the author redraws the paradigm of church leadership back towards a shepherding model. This really helps when dealing with the failings of people, but at the same time directs us to continue to be leaders.

is simply the hardest on the pastor's soul. Unresolved conflict drains you of your emotional energy, it steals your focus so that you filter everything through it. It occupies your mental capacities and robs you of your creativity. But here we are talking about unresolved conflict. Conflict itself can be valuable for getting your church back on mission. It will take courage to face issues and people, but actually getting to the core of an issue and bringing it to a godly resolution is a good thing. It's a kingdom thing. Jesus often engaged in it and got stunning kingdom results. No-one enjoys conflict, unless they have sociopathic tendencies, but conflict is a reality that all leaders and pastors will face. We must never live in a paradigm that always equates conflict with something bad because it could well be that the conflict you engage in saves you, and your church. You are also saving the people who are yet to discover your church and need its ministry. Conflict resolution

Learn the value of conflict. Its value lies in that it gets to a root, or core of an issue that is stopping the flourishing of a person or a ministry.

will always take courage, and courage grows as we dig into our values, understand why we believe something deeply, and then allow the Holy Spirit to fire our values up into godly conviction and passion.

Learn the value of conflict. Its value lies in that it gets to a root, or core of an issue that is stopping the flourishing of a person or a ministry.

For some of us, it is not that we would never face conflict, it is that we don't have an organised system or method to deal with it when it arises. In the swirl of emotions and the knot in our stomach, it is wise to know that there are some objective things you can do despite these unwanted feelings.

Foundations to navigating conflict

There are four foundations to keep in mind when navigating conflict, these apply to all types of conflict and will help you stick to an organised system of dealing with any conflict if you base your approach on them. They are equal in value and application.

1. *It may be personal, or it may not be personal, but in all conflict don't allow it to become personal.* One of the hardest aspects of conflict is that we often take it as a commentary upon us. We take comments upon our leadership, whether it be about our church or its programme, as a personal approval rating. This is too much for your soul to bear. Even if someone intends something to be a personal attack, even on your character, that is their issue and not yours. You do not have to live in their perception of you. This is different to accepting personal responsibility when we need to. I remember a very tense elders' meeting where my style was questioned and the wisest thing that I did was to simply listen and apologise. I was sincere in my apology and tried to improve the way I came across, but I didn't make it about my value or worth. There are other occasions when people have legitimate concerns and questions. Although such criticisms might involve some of the activities you take the lead on, and even might involve your preaching or teaching style, just answer the question and don't make it about your approval rating. Every question and criticism is an opportunity to learn something, even if what you learn is that you are on the right track! Often criticism that is directed to you is actually not about you, it's just that you are the leader in the position to deal with it. It is true that you are invested in your ministry with your gifts and your energies, there is a large part of you wrapped in it. It will carry your stamp. But don't make your ministry an extension of your very identity. Your church can never be that, the identity of your church is made up of the various people and ministries that everyone brings, and as such its true identity is as the body of Christ. You contribute and serve into this body. Don't make everything that happens in your church and ministry about you personally. Try as you might some people may never like you. This can be true if you inherit a ministry from a much-loved predecessor. Whereas it is always appropriate to try to be personable and professional, their liking you or not is secondary, even though this can be hard to take. Move past it and focus on the mission. Even when it seems to be personal to you try not to focus on this. Understand that not everything is actually personal it can be directed at you but borne out of an underlying frustration with other things.

2. Approach conflict through the lens of your mission. The primary questions in all conflict is whether it will derail the mission or bring new opportunity to the mission. Reminding everyone involved what we are about whilst at the

Whilst everyone around you might be caught up in the drama or personalities of a conflict, you have to keep your eyes on the mission.

same time acknowledging their feelings will go a long way in taking the heat out of many conflicts. The person that needs to remember this most is you as the leader. Whilst everyone around you might be caught up in the drama or personalities of a conflict, you have to keep your eyes on the mission.

3. Watch for patterns. Respond to repeated occurrences that are destructive. Don't be reactive to events. When you identify patterns, this helps you to shepherd and grow people. If you are only mission focussed you can become detached from what the real target of the mission is about. It is always about people! As a young pastor I was thrilled at the turn out to our painting party to decorate our church hall. I had hired decorators to do the ceiling and all the high parts of the church and the congregation really responded to finishing it off. Although my choice of colour did cause some comment everyone was on board and happy. I noticed one of the elders taking people aside and giving out specific ministry forms that we had not agreed upon. I focussed on the painting. We had a great time. Later that month I learned that the same elder had been meeting with others to build this ministry. I was then able to have a conversation on why this was being done on the side, because it had become a pattern. Even though this individual had even said to the people that there was no need to tell me, I didn't take it personally and was able to help the elder see that working together was far better than building something as an enclave within the church. If fact I was able to improve the ministry he sought to establish. More importantly, I was able to teach him a vital lesson in how the culture of our church should work and disciple him into being a team player. Identify and try to understand patterns and it will give you more authority to work through underlying issues. However let me quickly add, did you notice in the example I gave that it was a pattern of two occurrences? Don't leave a pattern so long that it develops into an unreachable stronghold. Don't leave a pattern too long by giving into fear. It will take courage to confront some things, but courage grows when we know why something is right to confront. This is when we confront from our values and not just because something has annoyed us. Confrontation should always be value based rather than a reaction. Courage to confront becomes easier when it is fuelled by the deep-seated values and well thought out convictions of what you know the preferred future of the mission is.

4. Define roles and policies. Give special attention to the roles of elders and leadership teams. Assumption and lack of boundaries is the environment in which conflict lives. When clear expectations are not set for our volunteers who serve in our church ministries, there is always potential for a conflict to arise as people overstep the intended role. Most pastors recruit relationally, in fact the gift of many shepherds is that they can get people on board and involved. What we need to understand is that initial recruiting from our personal chemistry is only the first step to real involvement. Every ministry that you have would be served by having a written role description that is taught and described before someone takes up the role. It will save a lot of heart ache later.

Elders. (Leadership Team). The scope of this book is not to do a detailed analysis of the role of eldership, but as far as reducing conflict and soul pressure is concerned it is really important that all concerned come to a working model of what the role of eldership in a church is there for. So that we can generate a healthy starter conversation, here is a functioning model that might clear the way for many.

Why we do things is presented by the pastor, discussed through scripture and agreed by pastor, ministry staff and elders. Most of why we do what we do is laid out in scripture and therefore the pastor and the elders can describe their values behind their mission and actions together. Why we do evangelism is a relatively easy answer from scripture that each leadership team can enjoy coming together on. To start here brings a foundation of unity.

What we do is largely the decision of the pastor presented to the elders. The pastor is the lead vision carrier of the church and therefore needs the freedom to set the direction and programme of the church. This does not mean to say that others cannot refine and shape this vision, or that other people cannot present ideas and initiatives, but the 'what' should be largely driven by the minister. When elders feel they should set the programme, a great failing is that the execution of the programme is largely not done by them, and therefore it is a once removed delegation of effort. It works better if the pastor is allowed to set what the church is to do in that season. Obviously, this is not done without consultation, checking of ideas and appropriateness of plans.

How and when things are done is with the strong partnership of eldership wisdom and advice. Elders can have a great role in actually achieving the vision set by seeking to make solutions as to how things get done in creative and innovative ways. Most pastors are probably on a quicker timescale for when something can be achieved, and it is the elders who can bring a slowing of things to a more reasonable and appropriate time scale.

If leadership teams could coalesce around this model of the 'why' being worked out together, the 'what' falling largely to the pastor, and the 'how and the when' being done in agreement together, much of the underlying conflict on leadership teams with elders would evaporate.

Elders can also be meaningfully involved in pastoral care and the insight to the overall health of the church along with the oversight to the general function of the church. A vital role for elders is to help write policies and guidelines that the church will operate by. The pastor is unwise to, and indeed should not be allowed to, operate in a vacuum. Through consultation all leadership teams should write policies around the boundaries on spending money and inclusions into ministries. When polices are agreed upfront, exceptions can be talked through reasonably. Policy writing protects the pastor from a reactive leadership, because she or he can simply refer to the policy that is already agreed. Policy writing stops everything being personality or current opinion driven.

A process for dealing with Conflict: Conflict navigation tool

Because conflict is inevitable, we all need a system of how to deal with it. Because conflict often involves deeply felt emotions, we need an objective system of how to navigate through it. Because conflict often brings with it the accusation that leadership is acting unfairly or is self-serving, we need a transparent system and process that those involved can see is being followed. Because conflict can become a muddled fog that derails our ministry, we need a map to lead us through the confusion of it. Because conflict causes fear and procrastination in facing it, having a guide and a tool to use can give us the courage to face it step by step. Because conflict is one of the main reasons pastors leave the ministry, it will serve us to have a clear way of navigating through it. And because conflict can be one of the major causes of damage to the pastor's soul and inner health, it is important we have a clear pathway to navigate through it to the other side. Here is the good news, there is always a way through every conflict and a new future on the other side!

> Conflict is one of the main reasons pastors leave the ministry, it will serve us to have a clear way of navigating through it.

A five-stage process of conflict navigation.

This is a systematic process that can be easily followed. The order in which it is laid out is important because each stage facilitates the ensuing stages. This process is so designed to help you know where you are in the whole conflict scenario. As you complete one stage you can then confidently move to the next and on towards a resolution. Please read the explanation of the process before using the navigation tool. Please use and print the navigation tool[7] so that you can keep a written record of the process which will in itself help you navigate clearly through the situation and bring clarity of thought and action.

1. Clarity -define the issue.

Before making any decisions, it is vital that you understand what the underlying issue of the conflict is. Don't move beyond this stage until you know what you are dealing with.

---

[7]You can download a printable version of the navigation tool from www.pastorssoul.com

This will involve fact finding and gathering. This is different from the following conversation stage because although the talk is sensitive and done in an understanding manner, it is for facts and reporting of information. It is not solution based at this stage. In getting a good understanding of the issue there are several important clarification questions that will get to the core of what the issue is -

a. What is the history of this issue? Is there a reoccurring pattern or a historical event that you need to understand that gives context to the current situation? Are there historical relationships that need to be taken into account?

b. What is the mission of the church or ministry? Refresh yourself in what the current emphasis in the mission of the church is, so that the issue is seen in light of the mission. Issues can cloud mission, but at the same time they may shrink in light of the mission that is being achieved.

c. Who are the people involved and what are their roles? There may be people involved who don't need to be, but an assessment of everyone's contribution will bring clarity.

d. How critical is this issue? Some issues, although they are important, are not mission critical and therefore can be handled slowly, or not at all. In gaining clarity there needs to be a definition of the size of and the importance of this issue. Some people may have been terribly upset, but the actual nature of the issue is non-critical and therefore can be handled at an easier pace. However, let us be clear that any upset is still important even if the issue is not.

2. Conversation -who needs to talk to whom?

This stage is to quickly engage all the people who are actively involved in the issue and the conflict. This is the type of conversation that involves understanding and listening. It is at this stage that the ground rules for any conversations need to be set. For example, 'Everyone gets to speak, and everyone gets to listen.' It is vital at this stage that you do not allow or indulge in triangulation. That is, that you do not allow people to talk on behalf of, or about people without giving the person who is being talked about the opportunity for direct communication. It is also vital at the conversation stage that you as the leader of the conflict resolution speak to everyone and do not receive all your information from only one source. The way some people report or talk about things can be overly negative or too positive, so it is important that all people are consulted and heard. It is in the conversation stage that you would wish to affirm the worth of all people involved in the conflict, even if you cannot affirm behaviour.

3. Consideration- Thinking and reflection.

Conflict can happen quickly but quick solutions usually don't resolve things and so a time of reflection and thinking is needed. This is also the stage in which you as the leader in the conflict would want to reflect on your personal feelings about the situation. As the leader, if we are angry or extremely disappointed, we will find it hard to resolve the issue in an even-handed way. One of the important commitments at this stage is to make sure that you do not cut the process off prematurely. What can happen is that because you have talked things through with several people already, you can be tempted to indulge in quick or half-hearted solutions. Instead of solving on the hoof, we need to ask, 'What are the consequences if this issue remains unresolved?' By asking this, you commit to finding the real and best solution. It is at this stage we begin to form what we might think is an answer to the conflict, but as we do, we need to check if we need more information. We need to check if there are others from either outside the situation or other people involved that we need to consult with. It is at this stage that we might seek advice or counsel from a mentor. There may be a need to go back to the conversation stage to bottom out the dialogue between parties and affirm further. Once this is done, along with trusted advisors, you can emerge from the consideration stage with the formulation of a plan to move forward.

4. Cooperation-agreed actions.

As a plan is formed it is tempting to broadcast it. This usually comes from our sense of relief. However, it is best not to communicate until all parties agree to what actions they will take in order to follow through with the solutions to the conflict. Conflict resolution has to be solution based and action orientated. Too often we can settle for an uneasy truce that causes no more trouble. This is not conflict resolution but keeping the peace, and this type of peace will not last. It is important at this stage to get everyone to commit to actions and make clear who will be the decision maker if there are decisions to be made. Most decisions can be made in consensus, but if as the leader you have to call something, because you have followed this transparent process, people usually will accept your right to do so. If they don't, they probably would not have co-operated no matter what. It is important that the others who are involved will have observed that you have at least followed a process. For best practice, the agreed actions should be recorded in writing or in some sort of minutes to a meeting. This can prove invaluable to the leader later if people seek to renege on their intended commitments. A good practice is to send an email to all concerned listing what actions are to be done by whom.

5. Communication-express your communication for the way forward in terms of the mission of the ministry and that the message is in language that is positive and agreed.

We need to let everyone know the decisions and the agreed way forward. Communication however needs to be planned and honouring to the people involved. It is wise to ask if there is a group or person that needs to understand the way forward before things go on general release. It is also wise to agree what language and message is to be sent if several people are going to communicate to those in their areas of responsibility. Communication has to also inform of actions to be taken, people need to be assured that real change is under way. Communication has to be uniform so that there is no unpicking of old wounds or exaggeration. The goal of the whole process is healing and forward momentum and the way we communicate our solutions and actions will be key to this. We should always try to communicate real positive change, not just 'we are glad that is over'.

Please use this as a system to begin to develop your style of conflict resolution.

Conflict Navigation Tool

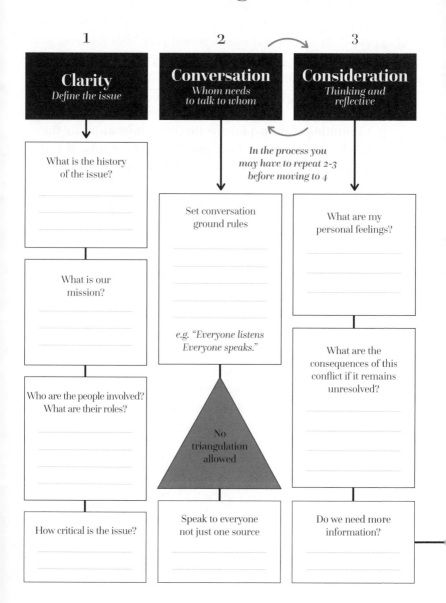

1

Clarity
Define the issue

What is the history
of the issue?

What is our
mission?

Who are the people involved?
What are their roles?

How critical is the issue?

2

Conversation
*Whom needs
to talk to whom*

Set conversation
ground rules

*e.g. "Everyone listens
Everyone speaks."*

No
triangulation
allowed

Speak to everyone
not just one source

3

Consideration
*Thinking and
reflective*

*In the process you
may have to repeat 2-3
before moving to 4*

What are my
personal feelings?

What are the
consequences of this
conflict if it remains
unresolved?

Do we need more
information?

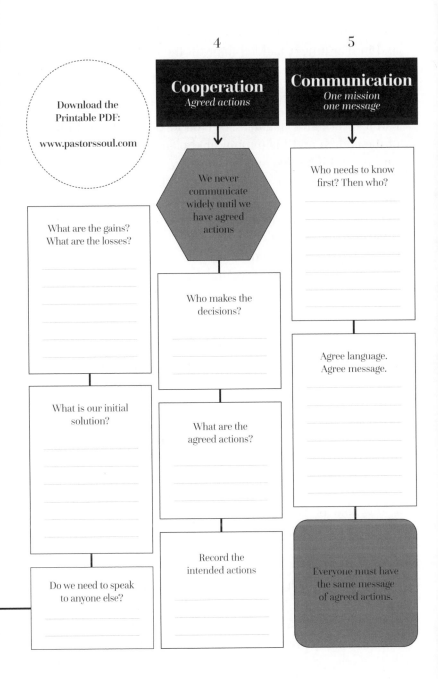

4

Cooperation
Agreed actions

5

Communication
*One mission
one message*

We never communicate widely until we have agreed actions

Who needs to know first? Then who?

What are the gains?
What are the losses?

Who makes the decisions?

Agree language.
Agree message.

What is our initial solution?

What are the agreed actions?

Record the intended actions

Do we need to speak to anyone else?

Everyone must have the same message of agreed actions.

I had been at one of the churches I pastored for over twelve years, and in that time, I had led many of the existing congregation to the Lord and we had worked together the see the church flourish. We did not so much have formal church meetings but more family nights to sort out our church business. We had tea, cake and laughter as we decided the intended future of the church and I communicated plans and dreams. It was fun. When I inherited another ministry, I assumed the church meeting would be the same and I was relaxed going to my first one. I assumed it would be a family time. It quickly descended into war! Criticism was aimed at some of the simple changes we had made and factions in the church emerged. I answered everything as politely and forthrightly as possible, but this was not the family meeting I assumed it would be. It became so aggressive that one of the assistants thought I would resign the next day. It was a nightmare! People who did not even attend the church came to have their say!

Underlying lots of conflict is the ongoing culture of a church. The new ministry had had far too much transition and the church members were upset at the turbulence of the years previous to my arrival. Any change I made would have been one change too many in a long line of upsetting changes for them. I learnt really quickly that I had to give myself to the

Underlying lots of conflict is the ongoing culture of a church.

rebuilding of a culture, a culture of harmony and respect. I learnt that this would take time. If you want to lead a ministry that is not lurching from one conflict to another you have to give yourself to the longer-term creation of culture. This is done through the teaching of fresh ideas, spending time with people and explaining changes kindly and carefully. As you respect people they will eventually come to a place of trust, but it takes some time. If your soul is to be healed from the wounds of conflict, direct yourself to the building of what you see is Christ orientated culture. You will not achieve this unless you make the deeper soul commitment to stay for a while. If your soul is bruised, reflect on what culture you want to build and think though the ways you can achieve it. This new focus will begin to heal you. Your soul as the pastor needs a plan and a system... and you need to give yourself time.

Thoughts for reflection

- What do you find the hardest thing about conflict? As you reflect on this, does it reveal any areas in your life that might need a measure of healing?
- What is your relationship to other leaders? Do you have a local leadership that needs definition around their role? How can you start a discussion on this?
- The early church had its share of internal conflict. **Read Acts 6:1-7 and Acts 15.** Can you identify some of the good things they did to navigate these conflicts? What was the main reason for the breaking down of the partnership between Paul and Barnabas?

Chapter Six

Work on your Wellbeing

I am part of a learning community, and so myself and our team spend several days a year working through topical issues of church life and development. During the 2020 pandemic, like most other things, it was postponed and then refashioned to be online. When our learning community meets in person it is well organised, has great surroundings, good content and the catering is of a high quality. So, for the online experience I decided to make an extra effort to make sure that we as a team had a comfortable room where we would not be disturbed. Like your church, my church campus can be flooded with people traffic, and so I was concerned we would be continually interrupted by our foodbank donations and other visitors. I had the room set up with comfortable seating, snacks and drinks, coffee and tea on tap! We were ready. I told the staff we would provide breakfast for when they came in and we would order lunch in. I was trying to replicate the experience of what they were used to for the learning community. Then came the day. I usually have a team effort on providing catering etc, (that's a senior leader's way of saying others usually do this part!) but on this day I wanted to model servant leadership and so assured the staff not to worry, I would pick up the breakfast bacon rolls. I set off on my cycle. The traffic on that morning seemed to target me and I had several near misses, but undeterred, bacon rolls in hand, I arrived at my perfectly planned, online, replicated learning community team day. I was actually feeling quite chuffed at myself for being such a servant. As I stepped through the doors of the church I was greeted with 'Mark, we have had a break in'.

But it was no ordinary break in. The perpetrator had sneaked behind one of the staff and followed right behind them in through the coded door. When questioned, the thief said he was working in the building and the staff member innocently let them proceed. Then when challenged by another female member of staff on the next floor the thief became aggressive and threatening but marched off in the other direction. The thief was eventually challenged by another member of staff, who, not knowing the intruder had a laptop stuffed under his coat, escorted him outside to an accomplice. They both made off. So, I arrived into an incident in which three of the staff were shaken and agitated and feeling they had been taken advantage of. My offer of bacon rolls seemed unimportant at this moment. The team were more interested in checking CC TV than the seminar we were about to take. The rest of the staff had now entered my idyllic room, that was not supposed to be interrupted, and a discussion of how such a thing could have happened ensued. My initial hopes of a good seminar and learning community seemed to be somewhere with the laptop under a jacket somewhere else in the city. Having checked everyone was ok, and made sure those threatened were not too shaken, we decided to settle to the day at hand. But the irony of this day is that the topic of the learning community was...wellbeing! Living calmly. Self-leadership. Boundaries. Leading from a good place. And my staff now had to sit through a first session on how to fill up their various emotional and life tanks and live balanced lives! They were still trembling and angry! But this is the point. Wellbeing cannot be something you occasionally visit; you have to have it in reserve, otherwise a crisis or event will rob what little you have. Wellbeing has to be something you routinely work on or invest in all the time. It has to be part of what you do because you never know when you need to call on the reserves it deposits in your life.

Some might react to the description 'work on your wellbeing' as

Wellbeing cannot be something you occasionally visit, you have to have it in reserve, otherwise a crisis or event will rob what little you have.

if it should not be work but more of a softer approach, but I use it because it has to be taken seriously. The work of wellbeing might just be the thing that ensures you actually are healthy enough to do any other work. It can save your career, your marriage and your key relationships, so let's leave it as 'work on your wellbeing' because if you don't you may never work. By the way, because of the reserves and maturity of the staff, they did get a lot out of the learning community day! The topic probably helped the shock of the morning.

The Hebraic mindset of the nature of our make-up is that we are one entity. We are a unified creation. Even the title of this book could be slightly misleading as if our soul is something that can be singled out from other aspects of our make-up. It can't. Everything about you is connected to everything else about you. This is not some Star Wars 'feel the force' concept. We are distinct from general creation, although we have an important interaction with it, but as far as our human design and make up goes, it is vital you see that everything is completely connected. Physical, spiritual, emotional, intellectual, relational, rational, soul, spirit, biology, or however we might describe ourselves. Everything is connected and affects all the other aspects of our make-up. We only use what seem like compartmentalised descriptors to help us understand and improve certain aspects of who we are. Too many of us don't get that we are interconnected beings. We think we can excel in one area and ignore good stewardship of another area. The first step to understanding wellbeing is to accept this interwoven nature of who we are. The bible actually describes us as being 'knit together', (Job 10:8-11; Ps 139:13-14).

> Everything about you is connected to everything else about you.

There are many approaches, and a vast amount of good material, dealing with the subject of human and ministerial wellbeing[s], too much for the scope of this book. But building on the understanding that we are this connected whole, we could see our lives as an interplay of the spiritual, the physical, the emotional and the rhythms we create around ourselves.

---

[s]God's plan for your Wellbeing – a 50 day guide. By Dave Smith Waverly Abbey Resources. Also see www.wellbeingjourney.org this is a good general guide to the interconnected nature of wellbeing and something to use with the congregation. Take the Day off by Robert Morris FaithWords (Hachette book Group) - more aimed at ministers and business people but for general use too.

Our interconnected lives

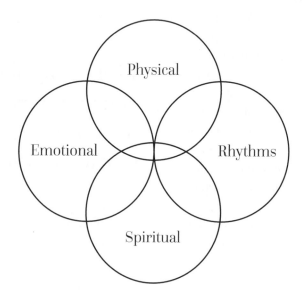

Even these categories are vast and so as a starter but also a timely and targeted word to you we are only going to investigate certain aspects of these areas of your wellbeing that relate to the pastor's soul. These are:

- **The physical** - the need for exercise
- **The spiritual** - your prophetic input
- **The emotional**- honesty with feelings
- **The rhythms** - Relax, rest and recharge and know the difference

These are not listed or dealt with in any order of importance.

The physical – the need for exercise

If we want to care for our soul and the inner person, we are going to have to take exercise. Reading is to the mind what exercise is to the body and none of us would consider never reading, or only reading when the fancy takes us. You are probably already convinced of the merits of exercise, whether you do it or not. You are probably not going to be found writing a message on why Christians should not exercise! But like regular witnessing, we all know we should do it and can encourage others to do it, but it often fades from our routine. So rather than extolling the virtues of the endorphin release to enhance your mood, (although we have made the point that everything is connected) or show the way that it clears the mind for sharper thinking, (although as said, everything is connected!) let us instead give you an easier way to get going in an exercise routine.

Before starting any exercise routine, it is wise to consult your doctor for a medical check-up. Your local health professionals can advise some of the ways or types of exercise that may or may not be the best for you. Having said this there is usually some sort of exercise that everyone can do, you just have to find yours. There are three principles to making exercise serve your wellbeing. First it has to be a part of your weekly schedule and be counted as important as any other appointment. It can be flexible, but it has to be there as something you do. It cannot be left to if you get around to it. For some, this will mean that you have a set time for it. For others, it will be a commitment to do something at least three times per week, and you are flexible about how you fix it in your schedule. If exercise is to do you good, it has to become a fixture. A second helpful principle is that it is good to link your exercise to a longer-term target. This might be a weight loss goal, or if you don't need to lose weight an overall distance goal, or time spent in exercise goal. Something that is longer term so that takes regular effort to achieve it. Something that takes up to a year to achieve. This will take thought and planning, and you will have to be reasonable. Don't plan to climb Everest or win the Tour de France, but plan something longer term that you can enjoy achieving. This can be as simple as doing one hundred walks, or one hundred hours walking. It's a longer-term target that you get done over time. Thirdly, have a weekly goal. This is a baseline minimum that you seek to do every week. You may do more, occasionally you may do less, but in the course of your weekly routine you check off this goal as something you have done. It could be something like run 10k per week and your overall target is to achieve 500k. It could be visiting the gym twice per week and walk once. It could be simply an amount of time each week regardless of what you do. It is whatever works for you. Routine, longer term targets and weekly goals help us keep exercise in our weekly lifestyle because we all know that ministry can throw up something unexpected which can be very challenging to our scheduling. Of course, you may not need any of this because you just enjoy getting out there! If that is you, just go with the flow!

For the spiritual ones who have not skipped this section, there is an important principle of not allowing your body to rule you but to serve your spirituality. You will be surprised how spiritual clarity, ideas for messages and talks, clarity in important decisions all come whilst you are exercising. Remember the road to Emmaus, your heart can burn too as you walk along! Don't underestimate this. For older ministers there is also a cultural moment to observe. Over the last two decades there have been two growth arenas, which for many have become the 'third space' away from home and from work. One is the coffee shop, and the other is the gym. We miss connection with the millennial generation if we don't understand the importance of both. You don't have to join a gym, but exercise is actually a witness to the climate change aware millennial generation.

Nonetheless exercise should largely be done not for witness, but for our wellbeing. It's a gift to yourself. It begins as a discipline and, over time, becomes a delight that you miss when it is not there. I would also make a plea that part of your exercise is in the fresh air, and not just in a room. Fresh air is more than fresh air, it's a reminder that it is God that gives us breath to our lungs.

The Spiritual – your prophetic input.

As the prophet Samuel comes on to the scene in the story of Israel 'The word of the Lord was rare; there were not many visions' (1 Sam 3:1). As Samuel receives his call, and Eli realises the baton is passed on, there is a subtle symbol that the revelation connection is back. Samuel, 'opens the doors of the Temple' as if to let the Word back into the heart of the spiritual journey of Israel. We need to open the door of our lives to let in the direct and now word of the Lord to us. Our soul needs prophetic and inspirational input. If all of our ministry is swallowed up into what we should do, or what we have to do to keep the programme going, our soul will shrink. We need a 'must do' from the Lord. We need the lightness in our soul that marvels at the fact we get to do this. Inspiration will move us from should do to want to, because we are compelled to. Prophetic input will move us from have to and ought to, so that we lift our heart in thankfulness that we get to do this. There will be many general approaches to wellbeing that encourage a focus on you filling your spiritual tank. These general approaches are valid, but I want to strongly urge you to sharpen your perception of healthy spirituality from being judged not only by time spent in devotions, but more by hearing direction and inspiration given to you. It is important for us to seek; but it is vital for your soul to actually hear something. When was the last time that your soul was so moved by something that you knew you had to act on it? This is prophetic input. When were you inspired to develop an idea or an approach to your ministry that caused you to know that what you were hearing was more than a good idea?

> Sharpen your perception of healthy spirituality from being judged not only by time spent in devotions, but more by hearing direction and inspiration given to you.

That you were running alongside an inspiration that was not purely of your own doing? Your soul needs this for its wellbeing. Call it the touch of God, call it inspiration, call it the prophetic word of the Lord, but we need this in order to be healthy. This input can come in varying levels of intensity, and we all routinely do things from a general devotion that we know is pleasing to God and others. I don't need a word from God to be kind or give encouragement to others. But my soul and yours does need regular inspiration. There needs to be a voice to your soul that connects you to God. We all need to know what God is actually saying to us in the season we are in. We have made too many excuses not to hear what God is saying to us in the now moment. We have advocated general devotion and healthy habits of spending time alone with God as if that is an end in itself. The wellbeing of your soul needs a touch from heaven.

We are very subjective in the way we hear from God but we all would agree that this comes through reading the Bible. But we have to read with the goal of hearing. There is virtue in covering the material and doing a plan of bible reading, but there is more virtue in reading in such a way that you allow the bible to begin to read you. This means an openness to what God might be speaking into your life. You need to stay sensitive to what you think is being spoken into you for your season, it's this type of inspiration that will keep you.

Prophetic input often comes through honest conversation around issues that are important. This is why it is vital to have friends or spiritual partners who can engage deeply with you. When was your last honest conversation? Remember Emmaus, it was as they talked on the road that prophetic awareness came. Who is walking with you on your road so that you can really discuss the things you need insight into?

Inspiration will come when you ask the questions that you have. Jesus used questions to open up insight. God has placed some questions in your soul for the reason of speaking to you. God doesn't always answer these questions, but he uses them to keep you seeking and hearing. The asking, seeking and knocking prayer teaching of Jesus, (Matthew 7:7) is not just about getting things but probing more deeply into the questions God has placed in our lives. As revelation into these comes, progress is made.

For others, our soul is awakened by a cause that burns an impression into our inner lives. For some people, there are causes that are more than benevolence or a good charity, they are the way they hear the voice of God in their lives. The cause becomes the prophecy. Don't be afraid to follow the need in your life to advocate for something, this might well be the prophetic air that your soul needs to breathe. You can tell if a cause is becoming such in your soul because you compel and convince others to join you, rather than condemn them for not joining. Your prophetic cause gives you joy and breaks your heart. It is a burden that brings life to you and you can appreciate others are not carrying it.

Your soul need this wholly other prophetic input for its wellbeing. Where is your prophetic inspiration coming from?

The emotional – honesty with feelings.

Your feelings are a marker to an issue that you believe on the inside. Your feelings tell you something of what your perceptions are. Your perceptions may be false and thus generate inappropriate feelings, but nevertheless your feelings are the evidence that there is something you think is real. It is important that we are honest about our feelings and admit we have been feeling something for a while. When we are honest in this way we will get to the issues and as we deal with them, consequently we will lift our wellbeing. Denying our feelings is something we have all trained ourselves to do for the sake of appropriateness, but eventually we have to own them, and admit them, if we are to resolve them.

Our feelings also project more than we think. We think we are hiding them, and some of us can do this better than others, but consistent hidden feelings do not remain hidden. One of the greatest needs of pastors is to become self-aware, to know how they are coming across to others. If we are not honest about our feelings and don't learn to resolve them, we become further and further detached from how we are coming across. We think we are the same, but your unresolved feelings are changing you. They are adding an edge to your answers. They are changing the expression on your face. People who have known you for a while can detect that you have somehow changed. You think you are acting the same, but your unresolved feelings act like a cloak to you and a window to the watching world. The whole discipline of emotional intelligence (EI) is how we track and admit our consistent feelings, so that we can appropriately live well with ourselves and come across to others in a way that serves and enhances them. It is important for our soul that we track our mood.

> You think you are acting the same, but your unresolved feelings act like a cloak to you and a window to the watching world.

Some of us have lived in a mood that is fuelled by an internal issue for so long that we have come to accept that this is just the way that life is. But if we would take the time to track our mood and ask the question of what the issue behind it is, we would see our wellbeing flourish. We need to be aware that there could be some underlying issues that are casting a mood or a set of feelings in your life. The more you ignore or don't admit this mood, the less you will address the issue that is an illegitimate resident in your soul. It's time to admit your feelings. You can do this by tracking your mood. You can track your mood by looking at the patterns of your feelings. You have to admit what are the dominant consistent things you are feeling. Everyone can have a day when they are feeling low and usually, we know why this is. But some of us live with a mood. It's close to the surface but not quite at the surface, and we never take the step of honesty to admit it is there. It's within these consistent patterns that we can find a way to best understand ourselves. Are we consistently frustrated for no apparent reason? Are we bored or detached often? Are there people we are consistently avoiding? Do we lack motivation? Or are we consistently looking forward, full of motivation? Do you have a level of anxiety all the time? What is really on your mind when all other distracting thoughts are removed? What is your persistent thought pattern?

In all of these consistent moods there is an underlying issue. It may take help from someone for you to uncover this, but there is always an issue to bring to the light. One of the key questions you will have to answer concerning your underlying issue is whether it is out of your control to solve it, or is there something you can do to resolve it? If it is beyond your control you can begin to release it to God's grace in prayer and take a higher perspective on life. If the issue is within your control you can carefully make a plan to deal with it. Here is a way of tracking your mood or emotional patterns.

Mood Tracker

At the same time each day of the week for the month track your mood.
When you have done one week see if you can see a pattern.

Monday

Strong	Confident	Anxious	Bored	High	Why?
Creative	Energized	Fearful	Weary	Medium	_____
Happy	Expectant	Frustrated	Depressed	Low	_____

Tuesday

Strong	Confident	Anxious	Bored	High	Why?
Creative	Energized	Fearful	Weary	Medium	_____
Happy	Expectant	Frustrated	Depressed	Low	_____

Wednesday

Strong	Confident	Anxious	Bored	High	Why?
Creative	Energized	Fearful	Weary	Medium	_____
Happy	Expectant	Frustrated	Depressed	Low	_____

Thursday

Strong	Confident	Anxious	Bored	High	Why?
Creative	Energized	Fearful	Weary	Medium	_____
Happy	Expectant	Frustrated	Depressed	Low	_____

Friday

Strong	Confident	Anxious	Bored	High	Why?
Creative	Energized	Fearful	Weary	Medium	_____
Happy	Expectant	Frustrated	Depressed	Low	_____

Saturday

Strong	Confident	Anxious	Bored	High	Why?
Creative	Energized	Fearful	Weary	Medium	_____
Happy	Expectant	Frustrated	Depressed	Low	_____

Sunday

Strong	Confident	Anxious	Bored	High	Why?
Creative	Energized	Fearful	Weary	Medium	_____
Happy	Expectant	Frustrated	Depressed	Low	_____

After you have tracked for a month
ask if your mood is generally low/high
Is there a recurring mood?
What issues have you 'verified'?

Download the
Printable PDF:

www.pastorssoul.com

Week One	Main moods	Total highs	Total mediums	Total lows

Week Two	Main moods	Total highs	Total mediums	Total lows

Week Three	Main moods	Total highs	Total mediums	Total lows

Week Four	Main moods	Total highs	Total mediums	Total lows

The rhythms – Relax rest and recharge.

A rhythm is creating a time and energy environment around your life that grows your wellbeing. A previous way of thinking was to talk only in terms of time management, but modern research has included the idea of energy management[9] into the wise equation of life. Creating rhythms helps us manage the ebb and flow of our energy, as well as making priorities in our time. Clutter of activity can crowd our lives and so good rhythms are vital.

There has been so much written and said concerning reclaiming the theology and idea of building a sabbath into our lives that we don't need to go over it here. Although it must be said that, more than reclaiming sabbath personally, we have to learn to teach it well to others. But the idea and theology has been narrowed from its original intent down to a few activities of engaging in more focussed worship and getting some rest. This is adequate but it does not describe all that sabbath means. I liken some of the expressions of sabbath to what we have been noticing as weak financial stewardship. Some people tithe faithfully but use the rest of their money very unwisely. They expect that paying a tithe will act as a lucky charm over their lack of wisdom on the rest of their finances. It simply doesn't work that way. We are to be stewards and generous with all that we have, and tithing is only one part of a whole approach to managing our finances well. It's the same with an approach to sabbath. Some people think that taking a sabbath means that they can work in any way they please the rest of the week, so long as they crash for at least one day. It doesn't work that way

---

[9]For a clear description of energy management see https://hbr.org/2007/10/manage-your-energy-not-your-time And the work of Molly Fletcher in her book The Energy Clock (Ignite Reads) is a helpful tool.

and is a poor interpretation of what is meant by sabbath. It is better to have an overall approach to the rhythm of our lives that includes sabbath.

My favourite Scottish evangelist, Mark Ritchie[10], once used the illustration, that was probably not original to him, but it was from him that I heard it, that if your mobile phone is low in battery you don't place it in your sock drawer just for a rest, you have to plug it in for a recharge! It is the same with us, sometimes inactivity alone is not replenishing we need to do some things that actually fill our tank. Too often we have made our time off time just about rest. It is not, it's about replenishment.

> Too often we have made our time off time just about rest. It is not, it's about replenishment.

We need to create a rhythm around our lives that makes time and space for the best version of us. Alongside, and interwoven into our working life, we need a rhythm of replenishment. Replenishment involves at least three important aspects; I call them my 3 R's. First in order to replenish we need to **rest**. Athletes sleep well. They know the value of good rest. I know that it is well argued that some high-powered leaders only sleep for a few hours, but this is rare and is often more of a myth than it is truth. Your mind and your body, your emotions and your psyche need a shut down. It is a grace that God affords to us so that we can learn to trust that today was enough, or that the

---

[10] https://mark-ritchie.com/about

current situation is not solved all at once. There are occasions in times of crucial decision making that the best thing you can do is take a rest in the daytime before you carry on.

Second, in order to replenish, we need to **relax**. We need to do something we enjoy. We need to give time to something that engages our minds in a different way so that we can feel different things. The pastor's soul is involved in so many serious and thoughtful things so there need to be blocks of time that engage you in other things that lighten your mood and spirit. It is even healthier if you have several things that you enjoy and not get fixated on one mode of relaxation. Some of us need to have other ways of spending time with our wives other than the cinema! Relaxing actually heals a tendency towards guilt and self-effort in your ministry. Certain personality types find it difficult to relax because they are over industrious. The root of this industry can be an insecurity that they have to keep everything on track. The last time I looked the church belongs to Jesus. It's time for you to relax. Do something you enjoy. You can do this alone or with people you want to be with and don't just have to be with.

Thirdly, in order to replenish we need to **recharge**. This is when we do things that pique an interest. It can be learning a skill that make us feel better as a person. It is input into us that we feel is giving us something. This can involve learning something, but this learning may not be necessarily linked to your immediate role, although it might come in useful at some point. It can be something not related at all and you just want to know it because you enjoy knowing it. It can be a work-related seminar that you enjoy, the point is that it recharges you and gives you energy and personal development.

These three are to be built into your life rhythm, and not just crammed into an attempt at a sabbath day. A sabbath may include a version of all three. Sabbath should actually include worship, rest and replenishment in family relationships and as such can not achieve everything mentioned here. It is also true that there are some overlapping things between rest, relaxation and recharging and so we should not be under pressure to always distinguish between them. The point is we have to be more thoughtful in our view of sabbath and more intentional about rich and varied rhythms of replenishment.

When the disciples looked across the table at Jesus, they saw someone who was at complete peace with himself. When the Sadducees and Pharisees ganged up on Jesus to ask which was the greatest commandment, they did so from their perspective of score keeping. They were always striving to earn the next level of acceptance. Jesus answered them by saying they should be in love with God, express love to others, but also noted that our love should not miss out ourselves. Jesus told stories of unfair managers, who, having been let off their debt, began to choke those who owed them because they had nothing but a poverty of spirit on the inside. Our wellbeing isn't something to trivialise with the excuses that we are too busy. Our wellbeing is expected by the One we are serving. It's life stewardship. As we work on our wellbeing it connects us back to the One who is the real source of it.

Thoughts for reflection

- Fill out your mood tracker over the next week and month – what does it tell you and what action will you take?
- What is the issue that erodes your wellbeing the most?
- What are the biggest draining factors in your professional life? Is it a certain meeting? Is there any way that you can change this?
- Do you have a system of planning your time? (The final chapter describes an approach that might be a starter for you.)
- **Read 1 Samuel 30** The famous story of David avenging the destruction of Ziklag. Identify the themes of physical replenishment, emotional honesty and prophetic input that contributed to the noble way in which revenge was carried out and fairness to David's men was displayed. What lessons of wellbeing can be identified?

Chapter Seven

Serving from your Sweet Spot

Bob gave me my first significant opportunity in ministry. As the ministry leader he took a chance on me. The church he assigned to me had 21 people in it, two of whom left on my first Sunday[11]. The church had a house and a car that came with it. The house was 14 miles from where the church met. But it was a hard 14 miles through country roads. It took over 30 minutes to get there. The car broke down on it's second outing. The church was a Christian Servicemen's Centre outreach to the US military in the UK. One of the GIs offered to tow us back to the house so that we could get the car fixed. He had obviously never towed anyone before, because he set off at a pace that would have been respectable at the nearby Silverstone race circuit. Both mine, and my wife Kathy's heads snapped back, and Kathy had to steer through the idyllic countryside as if she was in a rally race. I just kept saying to her, 'Darling it's going to be ok but just concentrate.' She turned pale. Halfway through this ride, it did cross my mind if God had brought us out here in the middle of nowhere to kill us! We made it- Kathy was shaking all over as we got out! We thanked the GI for his kindness, and he went on his way. That ride became a metaphor for that church, it was a wild exciting ride. Although it was broken, it soon became a centre of hope and we saw over 130 people come

---

[11]It was a military church, and they were being reposted to another location.

to faith for the first time in the next four years. You too will have your stories about your first church. Stories of how broken it was and how much you had to fix it. You will also have the story of how, through God's grace, and a little bit of faithfulness, God has helped you fix broken things and turn something around. If you are still in the first phase of a new ministry journey, just wait, the change will come.

Though these types of stories help us in one way, yet in another significant way they don't. They help us because we can see how God can use us if we are willing. In fact, my main reflection on my time with the Christian Servicemen's Centre ministry is that God can do anything if you are willing. If a church is willing, God can use that sort of church beyond their expectations. On the other hand, these stories don't help us because, if we are not careful, they train us not to grow into our gifts but to rely only upon our serving effort. When Bob offered me this church, I thought he had offered me the highest privilege of my life. In fact, like me, you may feel the same. When we get a ministry opportunity, we cherish it. When you are offered something that is actually not in good shape, but you put your best effort into changing it for the better, it can be this very devotion and sense of privilege that will keep you working hard, but yet ignoring vital learning of how to grow into your sweet spot. We can get stuck in our 'effort at everything' spot. We all have stories

There are many things you can do, and you do many things well, but you are not gifted to do everything that you are responsible for.

of when we had to do everything, but then things changed over time. These stories are good for foundation and for a season, they are not good for our soul in the long run.

There are many things you can do, and you do many things well, but you are not gifted to do everything that you are responsible for. There are some things that you do because they are there to do and you have to do them. One of the pressures that builds upon the pastor's soul is the continual tension between our giftedness and our large capacity to serve at the general work of the ministry. For many years we have done many things that are not really ours to do. We have done them because we were willing to serve. This willingness has often worked against our effectiveness. We have done them because some of us have held things to ourselves. This could be because of insecurity or lack of training. We have done things because we simply had to. But for your soul's sake, you have to consider whether you are operating from the centre of your gifts. To use the golfing term, we need to hit from our sweet spot. Let's be clear, there is always a part of every ministry assignment that entails general serving. In the book of Nehemiah there were perfume makers and goldsmiths who helped build the wall. They were not gifted to do this, they just pitched in to meet the need of the hour (Neh 3:8). We will always have seasons where we must let the presenting need take precedence over our primary gifts. But this cannot be your ongoing ministry style. It is also true that we should not only empower others to help us because we simply don't like doing something. Equipping others has to go far beyond our need to work to our preferences.

Ministry is a fair interplay between your gifts and your devotion to serve at that which needs doing. For many of us we have not grown into our gifts because our devotion has got in the way. When we allow this to happen, we as the leader are blocking someone else's use of their gifts. This is the real price that our church pays.

> Your gifts and how you work them out in your calling will prove a source of healing within you. Conversely, frustrated gifts and blocked calling will bring soul weariness and inner damage.

You have been placed where you are placed precisely because there are some things about your situation that are broken, and it is your gift to put it right. It's broken and that's why God chose you. You are there to bring order to it and that's why God chose you. It is this realisation that leads me to say something very important for your soul. Your gifts and how you work them out in your calling will prove a source of healing within you. Conversely, frustrated gifts and blocked calling will bring soul weariness and inner damage. This is why it is important for you to grow past the 'giving everything a try' stage in your calling and commit to deepen and sharpen your gifts. A typical journey of ministry is that we have a narrow calling to start off with. Some even limit their calling down to one aspect of ministry by saying something like they are called to preach. Those of us in ministry know that the act of preaching does not occupy most of our time! Then as the ministry journey progresses, we enter a middle stage in which we tend to open out into a more varied ministry. This is because we need to learn and serve in a number of different roles. We take on pastoral counselling, we become platform communicators, we lead groups and even some worship leading. Some of us are responsible for the youth and children's work! We then learn to take on social projects and learn leadership skills and so the widening of our calling goes on. We do this because we are devoted and want things to succeed. Too many pastors stay here in this stage. We begin to empower others not because we really believe in using their gifts, but because we ourselves are too busy to contribute to the other area of need.

The latter stage of ministry is one in which ideally, we discover our deeper passions and motivations, and the gifts that rise out of them. In this stage you genuinely release people who have complimentary gifts to your own and can rejoice in the security that you are operating in your sweet spot. If you are in the latter stages of ministry and you are unhappy, frustrated and getting burnt out, the chances are that you are not operating in your gifts and you might feel trapped by the job you are in. The radical solution is to change your job. This may be the right step for you. Another solution is to make sure you find out and are clear on your gifts. You need to accept your gifts and bring others around you who are better suited to the areas of ministry that are not your sweet spot. In this way everyone gets to be successful. Your inner health needs you to be honest about your gifts and your interests. Your gifts release you, but they also limit you to a certain capacity. This is God's plan, because His dream has always been for the church to be a functioning body of interconnected people. If you want to really care for your soul and enrich your inner life, it is time to go on an honest journey of looking at your gifts. Be honest about what you are not good at. Be real about what you don't enjoy and what drains you. It's time to bring people around you. Your soul needs this. One of the best prayers you can pray is to ask God to bring the gifts and people around you who are the right people to help.

Sweet spot is one consideration, but what I call the stewardship spot is another. You can bring great care to your soul by simply hearing the words of the Apostle Paul, writing to the ones he was seeking to train:

> *"This, then, is how you ought to regard us: as servants of Christ and as those entrusted with the mysteries God has revealed. Now it is required that those who have been given a trust must prove faithful"* 1 Cor 4:1-2

Paul is making the point to us that there is great virtue in doing the job we have been set. Because you are commissioned to do a kingdom task, there is great healing for your soul in doing that task. This works on a personal integrity level. When we can look at ourselves knowing that all things being equal, we are working diligently at our ministry, we can live from a contented place within. Some pastors are unhappy in the ministry because they are secretly unhappy with themselves and their lack of performance. The reasons for this lack of performance may not be simple laziness. Lack of performance has many reasons, ranging from a lack of training to difficult interpersonal and organisational relationships. Whatever the reason, all of us will find soul fulfilment when we are confident we are making a strong contribution in our working life.

Being a diligent steward of our ministry also works on a spiritual level, because we are more likely to encounter the inspiration and leading of the Holy Spirit as we focus on our job. The inspiration of the Holy Spirit brings a richness to our inner life.

Being a steward of your ministry task also works on an organisational level because there are people who have put their trust in you to do the work required by the church. These people have normally committed financial funds to assist you to do this work and this is the trust we carry as pastors. When we carry our trust well, our soul responds with vibrancy.

A number of pastors, when they get into difficulty, look almost everywhere else to a solution instead of firstly seeking to press into a better level of their own ministry. Conferences and webinars are important and might be needed to upskill you in your calling, but they cannot be a substitute or an escape. Faithfully working through solutions as a practitioner brings a level of richness to our inner lives that is rarely matched by the latest seminar idea. Looking outside of our ministry should be to help to the practice of our ministry. We should not look outside for the latest distraction or exercise in leadership experience. It is important that our input serves the calling and the position we presently hold in this season. This is not to say everything we do is to be based only on a narrow view of the local church, but we tend to know when we are not focussed and not really being diligent in the stewardship we have been given. Be kind to yourself, but do make an honest assessment. Are the conferences and webinars you are engaged in an opportunity to upskill and stretch? Or are they a distraction from the time you need to focus on your local situation?

Another way in which we care for our own soul and get closer to our ministry sweet spot is to learn that we receive a great deal by investing and giving away to others. That was the difference between Stan and Luchen. Stan was a sharp and dynamic preacher who I really looked up to. I could not wait to go and hear him preach as I journeyed through my bible college days. He was my pastor. When he told a story in his messages you felt you were there in the action. He could make me laugh and the next minute I was in tears. I wanted to be like Stan. I taught in adult Sunday discipleship classes and ran a mid-week outreach for the church and so I came into some of the leadership meetings and the inner circle decision meetings for the church. I was too young to discern it properly, but in hindsight Stan acted like a brash CEO, made inappropriate statements in these meeting and acted as boss. His charisma pulled us along with him. Stan climbed a ministry ladder that again, with hindsight I have since concluded was not his to climb, and so there was a change of pastor at the church. Our new pastor was Luchen, who was not as sharp of a dresser as Stan! In fact Luchen, an older man, looked like a copy of Abraham Lincoln! He didn't speak like Stan either. He was simpler and not as dynamic. There were times the message was basic. He also would get excited at times and kick his leg out to the side! I was a little disappointed...at first. Luchen and his wife, Jewel, took seriously their responsibilities in the church and personally visited everyone. This was no mean feat as the church had 400 people spread out in separate communities. Luchen later set up teams of pastoral care visitors. Kathy and I had never had a pastor visit us before and our attic studio flat was complimented as if it was a New York loft apartment. When Luchen and Jewel left we felt valued and as if what we did mattered.

We were also invited to go and stay with them, which we did. Luchen told me stories of being a pastor and we talked for many hours about ministry. Kathy and I began to take trips with them, which, by the way, always began at 4 am! Luchen would get us up early to head into the morning, beat the traffic, have devotions on the way and taught us how to enjoy times with each other and God. When we wanted advice about how to be in ministry with a young family it was Luchen and Jewel we turned to. They drove all the way from Germany to the UK to see us just because they were invested in us. If you ask me now who shaped my life more between Stan and Luchen, there is only one obvious answer. But here is the thing, one of the last conversations I had with Luchen surprised me. Luchen and Jewel were returning to the United States and had finished their time in Europe. This was in the days before the communication tools that we have enjoyed the benefit from today and so their leaving felt more permanent. Luchen confessed that investing in us had given a new lease of life to his ministry. Our conversations had helped him think through the things he had done previously. By investing he had received. For me I felt it had been all one way, but for him it was a return investment. The same will happen for you. You can care for your own soul by consistently investing and giving a part of it away to others.

The opinion of what the job description of a pastor is can be as varied as the shapes and sizes that pastors come in! It seems that pastors are to be a cross between a business entrepreneur, a psychiatrist and a communication guru. Today pastors also have to be technology savvy and social media aware!

Some of us are confused as to what the job is that we are being asked to do and so how can we have a sweet spot in some thing we are not clear on?! Without adding to the confusion, let us go for simplicity. The role of pastors revolves around the three aspects of shepherding, leading and teaching. Shepherding being the nurture of people so that they progress towards spiritual health and life. Leading being bringing a sense of direction and collective working, with healthy systems so that the church makes progress together as a group. Teaching being a commitment to discipleship formation, declaring the gospel for outreach and a consistent teaching programme of spiritual realities that enable people to grow into their own destiny. If we give our soul to shepherding, leading and teaching, and bring gifts around us to compliment these things, then we can stave off some of the weariness that can attack our souls. Too many of us go beyond these core things before these core things have been adequately staffed or attended to. When these core activities unravel, then our ministry begins to become more of a burden than it should. When we add the clutter that comes with all the other expectations, it is little wonder that some pastors are too busy or lost in the fog of commitments and wonder what they should do next.

If you are going to get near to your sweet spot of working, you have to be clear on what your role is. Part of leading is knowing what you are supposed to be doing and then ensuring everything else gets done. Part of shepherding is making sure that as the work gets done people are growing and being nurtured in the process of doing the work. Part of teaching is providing compelling reasons for the work and strong healthy how to's of achieving the work. The more we study high capacity, effective, pastors and leaders, the more one sees that they are clear as to what they should fill their time with and don't allow it to be stolen from them. Many of us know this but then life happens, and we find ourselves well into the week, having been involved in all sorts of necessary things that needed doing and it fell to us to do them. Our dream of being the focussed person we want to be gets caught up in the urgent or because someone else dropped the ball.

You have to see time as an opportunity to make a difference and evaluate every use of it under this conviction.

Although I have seen this need for clarity for a long time, it was not until I changed my approach to how to view my time that I began to solve this dilemma. Lots of pastors want to only do what they are supposed to do, but because they do not have an intentional approach to how they see their time, they never quite get there. The apple watch is not a watch only, it is a management system for health. It offers

> In order to get to your sweet spot, you need clarity on what you need to do. In order to get clarity on what you need to do you need to believe in a system of how you use your time.

more than a clock on your wrist. Similarly, we have to have fresh thinking concerning our working week. We have to stop seeing time as slots to fill or to do lists to tick off. You have to see time as an opportunity to make a difference and evaluate every use of it under this conviction. We have to see time differently than just moments. There is nothing quite as fulfilling as feeling you have made good use of time, but this won't happen until you have a system of using your time that you believe in. This is more than time planning; it is the conviction to only give yourself to the things that are yours to do. In order to get to your sweet spot, you need clarity on what you need to do. In order to get clarity on what you need to do you need to believe in a system of how you use your time.

I only fill my working week with what I call my four P's. I do nothing else with my working time. I religiously only fill in my schedule around the four P principle. If something comes that is not in these categories, I don't do it but I ensure someone else does it. I do not allow any of these categories to become over stretched because even within them there is a temptation to make something fit that does not really fit.

The 4 P's stand for Personal, Programme, Projects and People. I don't do anything else with my time. Every week, before I fill anything in on my schedule, I think what I need for me personally.

The P of personal is the things that I need to do for me. This can range from spending more time with Kathy, to going on a prayer retreat, to booking a holiday. It's personal time. It's not just odd jobs, it tends to be things that fill me up personally.

Next, I look at what is fixed on my programme and see what preparation needs to be done for that. This might involve some problem solving. But I plan what needs to happen in the background to achieve the fixed things I am committed to.

Thirdly I give time every week to ongoing projects. My projects are usually from 90 days down to 1 month in duration. Longer projects are put into a category marked as 'other' and I work on them as needed.

The last P stands for people. Every week I think about who I need to spend time with. Within the people category I am careful not to fill that time with too many draining people. I am only sharing this with you to prove to you that I have an approach to time.[12] You don't have to copy it, but you have to have an intentional approach to time if you are to get to the clarity you need for your own soul care.

---

[12]You can download a printable PDF copy of this weekly planner at www.pastorssoul.com

Weekly Time Rhythm

Personal

Monday

Tuesday

Programme

Problems to solve

Wednesday

Thursday

Projects

30 days

60 days

90 days

Friday

Saturday

People

Personal:	Urgent:	Encourage:
Meetings:	Admin:	Other:

Sunday

If you don't have a thoughtful or intentional approach to your time than just filling in your time planner with commitments, why not take a step back and try a few systems out? Seek to arrive at an approach on how you use your time that comes out of your values and a clear understanding of your role.

As shepherd, leader and teacher, I don't do much else than this in my ministry life. I don't want to. I am clear on these roles for my ministry. I don't do all the shepherding that needs doing, I don't do all the leading that needs doing and I don't do all the teaching that everyone needs to hear, but I know that my time is used so that I am fulfilling the core roles of my life. My soul needs this, and so does yours.

The richness of your inner life will affect everything else about you.

The richness of your inner life will affect everything else about you. This is the message of this book. The state of your soul is already affecting the state of your ministry, so it is wise and imperative to care for it. You know this message; many have told it. I have tried to provide some practical insights and tools to help you in your journey into a healthier inner life. We should remember that the healthy pastor's soul is also anchored in our calling, our commissioning and our anointing and the strength that God provides. Techniques, insights and understandings are of little value without a clear sense of your calling, your commissioning and anointing. Our soul is buttressed by the grace of these spiritual realities. It is in that strengthening grace that I invite you to speak into your life the concluding convictions that I have often repeated to myself. These are...

By His grace, I will steward and do my ministry assignment well.
I will seek to finish every phase of my life well.
I will take as many people with me on this Jesus journey as is possible.

...these convictions will put something healthy into your soul.

I pray your soul be watered by God's Spirit as you live this ministry life. My prayer for you in this and future seasons is –

"May you be intentional about caring for your soul, by considering what turns your dial as pressure builds and what sort of issues erode your wellbeing the most.

May you spend time with God and listen to His promptings. That you would consciously filter your intake, so that you don't saturate your soul with things that hinder.

That you would consider the people in your life - who do you have that listens to your heart and soul? I pray God would grant you people you can journey with. That God would grant you the grace to invest in close relationships that deposit life and energy into you as you deposit life and energy into them.

That you would learn the value of conflict, and sail through a storm by going back to your basic skills and refresh them. May God give you the insight and courage to know that you are not gifted to do everything that you are responsible for. And I pray that through these intentional commitments that the richness of your inner life will increase and affect everything else about you."

In Him,
Mark.

Thoughts for reflection:

- Can you list honestly your primary gifts and interests?
- List the greatest hindrance to you operating in your primary gifts in your weekly schedule. How can you address this?
- Try using the weekly time rhythm. Try it out for three weeks and then evaluate your use of your time.
- Who are the main people you are investing in, in this season?
- Read through the accounts of David's followers known as mighty men, **1 Chronicles 11.** What role did they play in David's success? How did their gifts blend together for the Kingdom purpose? Who are your 'mighty men and women?' What do they bring to your ministry?

With a little help from my friends

What follows is the combined wisdom of some of my friends.
They represent the very best of a generous spirit to help others.
They are all active church practitioners and leaders.
Their wisdom embodies the words of the Proverbs

Plans fail for lack of counsel,
but with many advisers they succeed.
A person finds joy in giving an apt reply—
and how good is a timely word!
Proverbs 15:22-23

These are indeed timely words.
They are words in season for this season.

James Glass

Regional Leader Scotland and the North West (Glasgow Elim)

Keeping your soul in lockdown

A former captain of a submarine was interviewed recently on Radio 4. He and his crew had once spent ninety days under the sea. He was asked what he did to ensure that he and his crew stayed sane. He summarised his "sanity strategy" along the following lines: routine; breaks; conversation; and managing expectations.

My soul care strategy, such as it was, could be set out along those lines.

Routine

I'm a morning person. My spiritual disciplines are practised before breakfast!

Bible

During the summer months, some of my most refreshing moments were spent in the Bible early in the morning. In fact, I look back on some of those mornings in late summer as the most enriching in my history with God.

Prayer

I have used the Lord's prayer as my prayer template for many years. My prayer routine was enriched further when I rediscovered Larry Lea's teaching outline on the Lord's prayer.

I also spent more time praying in the Spirit. I happened to see a clip of an Indian evangelist who began his ministry praying in tongues for seven hours every day. I didn't pray for that long, but I did pray for long enough to be reminded that praying in tongues is a uniquely powerful way to pray.

Journalling

Journalling has not been a regular discipline I have practised. I use it like a piece of specialist equipment to help me sort myself out if I feel I am losing perspective.

Communion

I should also mention here communion.

Re-establishing our 9 a.m. communion service online a few weeks into lockdown, unexpectedly became an opportunity to receive from God as well as to minister to God's people.

Breaks

I did try to ensure I took my day off. And I took a couple of weeks annual leave.

Rick Warren's "divert daily, withdraw weekly, abandon annually" is great advice. I tried to do that, but I'm not sure I did it successfully. The initial extreme lockdown was weird. For six days of the week it felt like you were inactively active. Then, on your day off, you were trying to be actively inactive. Some weeks it was all a blur and it felt impossible to rest properly.

Conversation

I am one of those people who is fortunate to have good friends and close family relationships. I think one of the difficulties of lockdown was the lack of in-person fellowship.

Managing expectations

There was so much unrealistic expectation about what we were going to achieve personally and collectively in the early days of lockdown.

I was fortunate enough to be reading a book on Reformation church history at the time. They had epidemics, persecutions, wins and losses.

In the end, they just kept going, believing God.

I'm so glad we're no longer leaning on how many views we had on YouTube or Facebook. Hopefully, after seven months of what might be a very long time, we've learnt to lean on God. At least, I hope I have.

Duncan Clark

Senior Leader Coventry Elim

Without doubt, navigating the challenges of a pandemic has been one of my most significant leadership tasks to date. Like many church leaders, I first had to cancel or postpone many of the events, gatherings and meetings that I love, and then had to quickly learn how to plan, prepare and strategize in an ever-changing environment. Most importantly I had to figure out how to lead as a non-anxious presence; to lead from the overflow of the presence of God in me; to lead with wisdom and faith, not ignorance and fear.

For me, I've always been at my best as a leader when I have healthy, life-giving rhythms. When I start my day with spiritual and physical practices that fill my heart. It's old-school I know, but I need to start each day connecting to God in prayer, Bible reading, journaling; and then I run!

I've figured out that if my relationship with God and the pursuit of His presence is of primary importance, I must give it my fullest and most deliberate attention. During a pandemic that need has been even greater! Through experience I've learned that I won't drift into a deep relationship with God. It requires me to be intentional about adopting healthy habits that connect me in intimacy to God.

During the pandemic Psalm 131 became one of my favourite Psalms. It's incredibly short, but contains a vital truth:

> *But I have calmed and quietened myself,*
> *I am like a weaned child with its mother;*
> *like a weaned child I am content.*

In this Psalm, David is contrasting the experience of a nursing child with that of a weaned child. The nursing child wants to be in the mother's presence simply for the milk it receives, but the weaned child can find food elsewhere. The weaned child just wants to be in the presence of its mother for no other reason than intimacy and closeness. That's David's goal. Not to find himself in God's presence to get something, but simply to be with Him.

And notice what David has to do to get himself into that position: 'I have calmed and quietened myself.' In order to experience intimacy with God he must intentionally cultivate a quiet heart, mind and soul.

During the challenges of COVID-19 I've had to intentionally do that every day. In fact, a few times a day. It's incredibly difficult. My mind wanders. I think of the things I've got to do and the things I've forgotten to do. And then my iPhone calls my name. I become distracted by messages and media. It's not easy, but I need do it. The health of my soul is dependent on doing it.

And what do I actually 'do' during that time of calming and quieting myself? There's no rules. In fact, I tend to follow Henri Nouwen's simple advice: "Sit down and say, 'Lord, here I am.'" In that moment my soul finds some rest and I get a little bit healthier on the inside.

Jason Heron

Senior Leader Elim Northampton

Ecclesiastes 4:9-12

> *Two are better than one, because they have a good return for their labour: If either of them falls down, one can help the other up. But pity anyone who falls and has no one to help them up. Also, if two lie down together, they will keep warm. But how can one keep warm alone? Though one may be overpowered, two can defend themselves. A cord of three strands is not quickly broken.*

The above scripture has been foundational to protecting or enriching my inner life during this season of the pandemic. It is used at many wedding ceremonies to encourage those who are committing to marriage. It is used to say that healthy loving relationships are the key to success in marriage. Also, it reminds them that there is not only two in this relationship but three, that is God. I believe that healthy committed relationships are also key to help through every season of life, whether that be in work of ministry and life challenges.

Over this pandemic there is no doubt that my wife Lynda has been a great strength and help to me over every difficult situation including this current pandemic. Also, the foundation and strength that has enabled me to navigate through this season is the power of the Holy Spirit. I have received from and relied upon His faithfulness and grace.

Also, over this pandemic I have found there is a fourth strand to my soul care. This has been my friends and colleagues. During this pandemic season I can say they have helped encourage, strengthen and refresh me. This has been a lifeline to my wellbeing. There is no doubt that healthy relationships are vital to our navigation and success through every season including the pandemic. I would like to thank God and my wife, Lynda, and my friends and colleagues, who have helped me over this unprecedented season.

Mark Pugh

Senior Leader Rediscover Church Exeter

How I have Cared for my Soul

I've become all the more aware of just how delicately I need to nurture my soul. In the same way that I try to feed on a balanced diet for my physical well-being, I know more than ever of my need of a balanced diet for my soul. We may get physical energy from some foods that are not really good for us - likewise we can prop up our souls with 'food' that can be destructive.

During the national lockdown I learnt some key lessons about the diet of my soul.

Live in the present:

I'm a futurist. I love to dream of a new tomorrow and I've often fed my soul with a diet of concepts, strategies and hopes for the month and years ahead. During the lockdown a veil descended upon my future plans and I found that 'today' took on a new significance. I had become so accustomed to 'feasting on tomorrows table' that I had lost the recipe for 'todays meals'. I believe the church needs futurists, but my diet was unbalanced, and it was negatively impacting my soul. I have learned to create more space each day - to enjoy feasting on the now and celebrating the vastness of Gods goodness to me.

Rhythms are essential to good tunes:

All music needs a solid rhythm. Even complicated jazz scales and spontaneity require rhythm to make it beautiful; likewise, the 'tune' that flows from our soul needs rhythm. As an orchestra needs a conductor to keep the diversity of instrumentation in time, our lives need rhythm reminders and I've discovered the more complicated my life becomes the more I need them. Rhythm is ordered by God throughout the earth. The seasons come around with regularity, the earth spins consistently, the sun rises and sets with order and the tides of the seas can be predicted. Whether we look through a telescope or a microscope, we can see rhythms present everywhere and they are meant to be in our life also. I guard my sabbath, I take communion almost daily, I centre my thoughts and meditation around Gods word and I recognise without Him I can do nothing. I need rhythms that remind me of Gods goodness, His purposes, His empowerment. I need rhythms that dispel the ease with which I can slip into spiritual amnesia.

Physical activity and fresh air:

I remember a leadership coach advising me years ago to take regular short walks during my day - but what did she know? I packed my diary so tightly with back-to-back meetings that making such a change would surely make me less productive - but I was wrong. I wished I hadn't compartmentalised physical exercise as another to do item in my week. My soul needs the exercise as much as my body and I've had to prioritise this in my day. I find walking to be so good for me. I've bought waterproof clothes, comfortable shoes and have made a commitment to use the car less. It takes me longer to get to appointments on foot but when I arrive I they get a better version of me. The walk gives me opportunity to process, to declutter, to be grateful, to quieten my soul, to breathe the freshness of both the air and the Lord.

Leon Evans

Senior Leader LIFECENTRAL CHURCH

When this season of Covid 19 started I found myself using the phrase, 'this is not a sprint it's a marathon.' After a few months I changed that to, 'this is not a marathon it's a triathlon!!'

Just as I got used to running, I was handed a bike, then as I got used to cycling there was a lake to swim across! The result of so much uncertainty, steep learning curves, trying to navigate my own emotions and at the same time lead others through theirs was draining to say the least.

At the start of lockdown my mother died, the second week of lockdown our first granddaughter was born who we didn't get to see for 3 months. Then there was the loss of gatherings, human connection, traveling and other things that replenished me.

So, here's a couple of **don'ts** and a couple of **do's**...

Don't be afraid to be real - when God met Elijah on the mountain after his emotional and physical crash God asked him, 'what are you doing here?' Of course, he knew the answer, but he wanted Elijah to name things, in order for Elijah to be honest. Vulnerability is a key for emotional health, stop pretending, God knows it anyway.

Don't be afraid to ask for help - Erwin McManus says, "Your greatest strength is not when you can prove that you don't need anyone, your greatest strength is when you no longer have to prove you can do it alone"

During this season I intentionally leaned into my team, friends and mentors. As a leader it's not how hard we run it's the weight we carry when we run that causes the problems, (and I don't mean the pounds!) When we share with others including our team it's good for our soul and I think our sharing is good for theirs.

Do carve out time for "nothing" - by nothing I mean nothing 'productive'. Walks, silence, music, what John Eldredge in his book 'Get your life back' calls 'benevolent detachment'.

One of our problems is we look at Jesus' ministry and see action after action, event after event. What we fail to see is that in-between the action or event there were often 3 days walk! Time to detach, to connect and to reconnect. I found myself going from one activity to the next, one camera to the next, no time to detach and that's never good for your soul.

Do remember whose Church it really is - of course we know it, but do we really know it?

During this season I've used an app called the 'one-minute pause' developed by John Eldredge.

Every day I've surrendered my cares to Jesus, given everything and everyone to Him and asked him to restore the union between us. As I've done this bit by bit, He has brought life to my soul and reminded me the weight should never be on my shoulders, after all didn't He carry it all on His?

Paul Hudson

Midlands and North East Regional Leader

What have I discovered about
my soul-care during this pandemic?

Daniel in Babylon should have been in Israel, but he is with a people who have lost their way. Some of them have been released under the new ruler, Cyrus, but most stay as Daniel does. For the majority, life will never be the same again. As they look back, their failures and disappointments outweigh their successes and joys. Daniel has visions of the future that frighten him. It seems that life is going to get worse rather than better. He has visions that traumatise him of a world at war with itself. He has visions of Christ that break him like a shaking leaf. He has angelic experiences.

Then the words ... Everything is going to be all right!
(Daniel 10 v 19)

Horatio Spafford (1828-1888) was a wealthy Chicago lawyer, a beautiful home, a wife, four daughters and a son.

At the very height of his financial and professional success, Horatio and his wife Anna suffered the tragic loss of their young son. In 1873, Spafford scheduled a boat trip to Britain. Spafford sent his wife and daughters ahead of him while he remained in Chicago to take care of some unexpected last-minute business.

Several days later he received notice that his family's ship had encountered a collision. All four of his daughters drowned; only his wife had survived.

With a heavy heart, Spafford boarded a boat that would take him to his grieving wife, Anna, in England. It was on this trip that he penned those now famous words,

> *When peace, like a river, attendeth my way,*
> *When sorrows like sea billows roll;*
> *Whatever my lot, Thou hast taught me to say,*
> *It is well, it is well with my soul.*

These same words can be proclaimed over your life... Everything is going to be all right.

How have I found that it is well with my soul during this pandemic?

I have tried to stay connected in 5 ways and for the following reasons: -

Above – Christ and you are not where you think you are.

" *...your life is now hidden with Christ in God."* (Colossians 3 :1-3)

This circumstance does not have the final word over my life.

Side – Look to your friend.

" *...and they have proved a comfort to me."* (Colossians 4:11)

Paul, the theologian, who has revealed wonderful truths about Christ ends his letters focused on personal relationships. He shows us that we need both. We need to pursue Christ and pursue our love and care for one another.

Inside – Be thankful

"Jesus then took the loaves, gave thanks ..." (John 6 v 10)

You may not like who you are, your life shape, your age. You may feel insignificant and worthless. But give YOU to HIM, to the miracle worker. Give HIM your mind, your heart, your material things.

> *"Nothing can happen to me ... Sometimes when I stand in some corner of the camp, my feet planted on Your earth, my eyes raised toward Your heaven, tears run down my face, tears of deep emotion and gratitude."* (written by Etty Illesum, a Dutch girl in the 1930's who died in Auschwitz)

Below – Find the towel and basin

" ...He got up from the meal, took off his outer clothing, and wrapped a towel around his waist. After that, he poured water into a basin and began to wash his disciples' feet, drying them with the towel that was wrapped around him." (John 13 v 4-5)

The Son of God wrapped a towel around his waist and became a servant though one day every knee will bow.

Beyond – focus on those who walk out their faith in worse places

Paul realises that there is no place he can go where God isn't. *"I am a prisoner for the Lord"* (Ephesians 3 v 1)

My heart has been in Africa for 20 years and I am blessed to have friends there. There have been many times when I thought I was entering a non-sacred place only to discover I was about to discover something beautiful of the Lord. I found Him with the amputees of Sierra Leone; the persecuted of northern Nigeria and Burkina Faso; the raped of DRC; the prisons of Niger; the HIV stories of Eswatini; the famine of many nations; the slums of Kenya; the graves of Zimbabwe; the orphans of Malawi; the list just goes on. I have found Him in Prisons. Let me remind you again...

> *When peace, like a river, attendeth my way,*
> *When sorrows like sea billows roll;*
> *Whatever my lot, Thou hast taught me to say,*
> *It is well, it is well with my soul.*

We will come out of this pandemic and we will still in seasons find ourselves contained. I hope what we have learnt in taking care of our soul we will not forget. I hope we will know that everything is going to be all right.

Appendix: Do I need professional help?

It is quite common for pastors and leaders to avail themselves of all types of help in order to enrich their ministry. We have no problem having a leadership coach or a spiritual director. One of the ironic things is that many pastors act as pastoral counsellor to many but they themselves shy away from the thought of they themselves having a counsellor. Some how we have stigmatised the idea that there are occasions when the pastor needs professional help. Pastors tend to try to get their help through conferences and seminars, but there are occasions when sitting in a formal one on one setting with a trained counsellor would bring ministry and personal progress in a healthier way for the long term.

Not every reason to see a counsellor is for deep seated emotional or spiritual problems. Sometimes seeing a neutral person to talk through feeling or decisions is just simply some help to bring clarity.

What are some of the signs that we need to see a counsellor?

1. Are there reoccurring patterns or conflict or difficulty with certain types of people in your ministry?

2. Do you struggle with authority? Most pastors are free to lead in their own sphere, but do you find it difficult to take direction from Overseers, Bishops, or Regional Leaders, or your own local Elders?

3. Do you spend a significant amount of the day wondering how you will cope with your responsibilities? Does the thought and not being able to cope keep coming back to you?

4. Are you feeling overwhelmed?

5. Are there times when you disproportionately feel angry over something? In hindsight it was not such a bigger deal than you thought it was.

6. Are you continually fatigued?

7. Are you becoming socially with drawn? You cannot wait to be away for the meeting or social side of church, even beyond any natural introverted nature, you are struggling to be with people.

8. Are you at the stage of your career where you cannot work out what is next, and you would like some impartial advice?

These are just some of the reasons that seeing a counsellor might help you but for more resources and good articles please see **www.goodtherapy.org**

A helpful resource:

https://www.goodtherapy.org/blog/why-should-i-go-to-therapy-8-signs-its-time-to-see-a-therapist-0118197

Acknowledgements

Great thanks and deep appreciation go to my wife, Kathy, who has helped me craft the message of this book both as consulting partner and managing editor. Her insights and perspectives on its content have been invaluable and have helped shape its final form.

Kim Brindley counted it as a labour of love to proof read and organise the production of this project. Thanks for your diligence to my ministry over the last several years.

Julia Ayling acted as second editor. She has been both insightful and encouraging in helping me complete this work. Many thanks to you Julia.

I would like to thank my friend Mark Greenwood for his encouragement and advice in the production of this book. Thank you for your timely help.

Thank you, Jason Heron, for your continual encouragement to finish.

I cannot speak highly enough about Ruth Harris as the graphic and layout designer for this book. She just captures my thinking so well. Thank you, Ruth, for your hard work and excellence in your craft. Anyone reading this book should contact you for your services, www.ruthharrisdesign.com.

Thank you to my friends who have contributed to this book. Their collective wisdom is sharp and empowering.

Thanks to:

Leon Evans – Senior Leader LIFECENTRAL CHURCH

Duncan Clark- Senior Leader Coventry Elim

Paul Hudson – Midlands and North East Regional Leader

Jason Heron – Senior Leader Elim Northampton

Mark Pugh – Senior Leader Rediscover Church Exeter

James Glass – Regional Leader Scotland and the North West (Glasgow Elim)

Thank you to Chris Cartwright the General Superintendent of the Elim Churches in the UK who despite his busy schedule found value in this project to write a meaningful forward. Chris models care for the souls of the pastors under his care.

Please visit
www.pastorssoul.com
for all resources